Wealthy Moves

Build Your Empire, Own Your Time, Live Your Badass Dreams

Roota Mittal

Praise For Roota Mittal and *Wealthy Moves*

Roota Mittal realized that to make a living online, she needed to learn how to market her blog so it would get more views. She ended up using that marketing knowledge to quit a software job and her travel blog to create a multi-six figure freelance marketing business supporting beginners and high-end clients. Mittal's customers have made nearly $10 million in trackable revenue thanks to her help.

Forbes USA

If you are serious about changing your social media into a money-making machine, I highly recommend Roota!

Esther Inman, Founder Of 90 Day VA

The strategies in *Wealthy Moves* are the same ones that helped me go from zero to a multi 6-figure business owner. Roota is the real deal—no fluff, no nonsense, just pure execution-based wisdom. This is why she's been my mentor for 5 years!

Deepina Singh, Entrepreneur

Wealthy Moves is the raw, unfiltered truth about what it actually takes to build wealth and freedom from a business you're passionate about. This book will flip the script on how you think about money, success, and what's truly possible for you.

Sakshi Misra, Founder of Breakbull Advertising

Wealthy Moves is inspiring with a few genuine goosebump moments. The book does justice to the title and is relatable for someone coming from humble beginnings. I could FEEL a lot of things as I was reading through.

Preet Kaur, Launch Strategist

The highlight of the book for me was getting a detailed BTS of the last eight years of Roota's life and business through such a microscopic lens. Moreover, I felt relieved and happy to be reminded that every single thing I am doing right now is a wealthy move!

Chhavi Gupta, Founder, Breakfree LLP

Roota Mittal
https://learnwithroota.com/

Disclaimer

To Mom and Dad, who gave me the gift of dreams and the ability to chase them.

To Rachit, my best friend and partner.

To Kavya, my forever cheerleader

Table Of Contents

Introduction

I woke up sweating in the middle of the night. A nightmare had stirred me awake.

I was in my 40s, married, with children, living in a bungalow in an Indian city. My daily routine was that of a stay-at-home wife. It was the same thing every single day: doing everything for my family, for my kids, catering to my husband's needs and ambitions, and putting my own dreams on the back burner. I didn't have any creative control, any accomplishments of my own, any money to my name.

Sitting up in bed, I took a couple of deep breaths, trying to centre myself. It was then that I realized that what I had considered a nightmare was actually the reality of a lot of women I knew. The women in my own family: my grandmother, mother and aunts. I was lucky that I was born at a time when girls were "allowed" to go to school, have an education and pursue a career. But that was not a reality for most women at home. The men went out to work to provide for the rest of the family, all the money was in their hands, and there was a huge discrepancy in how much money the women were "given" every month to manage the household. I saw this firsthand, the women all around me felt like they had to dim their light to let others in their respective families shine brighter, appear smarter and successful. If these women wanted to take a trip, or buy a gift for someone, they were at the mercy of their husbands.

Even today, in most suburban families in India, the goal is to find and marry a "rich" husband. I remember the iconic singer Cher talking about this in an interview I watched online.
"My mom said to me, 'You know, sweetheart, one day you should settle down and marry a rich man.' And I said, 'Mom, I am a rich man.'"

I belong to a generation of women that wants to make their own money, save it, spend it, invest it, make more money, and build a bigger life without dimming their own light. I'm grateful that even though my mother didn't step out of the house and have a career, although she did have a side-hustle for a few years before my sister was born, she always wanted to make me feel capable and believe in myself to the extent that the world cannot deny me my dreams. I'm lucky that my father spent countless hours teaching me math and science concepts, teaching me important skills like time management, confidence, and public speaking. I'm extremely grateful to my parents, that despite their limited means, they sent me to dance classes and painting classes, had me join basketball camp, and countless extracurricular activities in addition to my studies.

I knew the sacrifices my parents made and I wanted to make them proud. But I faltered after I graduated from high school and made my way to college.

I went from being a straight-A, award-winning student, to getting a 4.7 grade point average in my first semester of my computer science engineering degree. It felt shameful, like I was a one-hit wonder, and my career which hadn't even begun yet, was nosediving at 30,000 miles an hour. I struggled to find my identity in college. I bunked lectures, I didn't qualify for the minimum grades that the college allowed to own a personal laptop.

At the end of the first year, I felt that I had disappointed my parents who had given me everything I needed to be successful. I was unfocused and had no goals and felt burned out after school. But I realized that I had to take control back of my future. So, I turned my ship around and graduated with a decent grade at the end of college, and with two job offers in hand: a Big 4 consulting firm, and a software startup. I chose to work at a software startup because they made me a pretty lucrative offer.

All my life, I had dreamt of making my own money and becoming independent. It felt like my life was finally starting. But two years into my job, I hit rock bottom again. I didn't feel like going to the office anymore, I was taking sick days, my mental health was deteriorating, while all my peers were getting promoted left, right, and centre. I felt like a failure. I felt suffocated and wondered if this was going to be my life until I retired at 60! Working weekends and late hours to solve client issues, building someone else's dream, being creatively unfulfilled even while you are making great money takes a toll on you.

I didn't want to feel like my potential was underutilized in the corporate world. I didn't want to work in a company for 40 years to finally enjoy my life in retirement. I wanted to live my most fulfilled life starting from my 20s. I wanted to own my financial success and not have it controlled by a boss or a corporate machine. At 23, I quit my well paying job without any backup options. I burned all the ships, set fire to bridges and jumped without a lifeboat. All I was armed with was a strong belief in myself, and some money saved that could keep me afloat for a year.

This book is about finding your ability to make money and own your financial future in the digital age. I want to show you how you can monetize your skills in today's economy and get paid handsomely for it. Your appraisals, bonuses, are in your hands now, not in someone else's. You get to control your topline and your bottom-line, where you work from, and how many hours you work every week.

Social media and the Internet have massively changed the landscape for women. Now, we don't have to feel guilty for our ambitions—we can choose our own career and work flexible hours, if we need the flexibility to take care of our family. Or we can go full boss babe mode, hustle and build a business empire of our dreams. Most importantly, we don't need permission and we get to do whatever we choose.

This book is a story and practical guide: from how I failed countless times to finally building a million-dollar business, got featured in Forbes International, and won an Entrepreneur Award called the '2 comma club'. Till date, I have served over 4,000 clients across 15 countries to drive more than 16 million dollars (and counting) in sales. In the process, I have built a community of 350,000 people. Additionally, I'm an angel investor for tech companies, and personally investing in real estate and the stock market to grow my wealth.

I know you don't care about all this though. You care about how this can help you. I believe there is a lot of bullshit in the entrepreneur world and coaching industry, and I'm here to help you get to the next level of wealth in your life.

I want to help you leverage your skills, your mindset and the immense power of the digital economy to build wealth for yourself and gain back control of your schedule. I'm taking you by the hand and I will teach you about sales skills, marketing strategies, leverage social media, creating a brand, getting clients from social media, closing high-end deals on sales calls, upgrading your money mindset, getting rid of money blocks and limiting beliefs, investing and growing your money—everything you need to know about building your own seven-figure business and becoming a CEO who makes wealthy moves.

This book is everything I wish someone had told me back when I was 21, about business, money and wealth. I might not be one of the most successful entrepreneurs and I might not have the biggest following. But I have written this book to share the mental models and life principles which have served me best till date to make money, generate wealth, solve problems in the world, get paid for it, and live a pretty good life.

Consider this advice, recommendations, stories, moves from your 31-year-old sis! Please note these are my experiences, and the advice is solely based on them. Take what you need, take some stuff with a grain of salt, and leave some stuff behind; please use your intuition to do that. Trust yourself. You know what you need at this point in your life, and you can revisit this book later to learn or implement something more later. I've also structured it in such a way that you don't need to read it chronologically to get value from it. If a chapter calls out your name, dive in and come back to the rest later.

There are a lot of terrible mindset beliefs that we've learnt from our childhood, or earned because of our adult trauma, or simply because life is heavy sometimes. But my goal is for all of you, ladies and gentlemen, or however you identify, to charge your worth, charge high-end prices, scale your million-dollar business, help thousands of people globally, and live a life that you're proud of.

My book is different because it is based on my journey of growing my business in the international space, especially as a woman in India. I did the damn thing to grow my brand and become visible and get clients. And I don't see a book in the market that guides today's 20-year-olds to build their own business by leveraging the digital economy. I come from a simple family background and I want to share the message that if I can do it, so can you!

I have devoured countless business books from industry leaders such as Russell Brunson, Alex Hormozi, Tim Ferriss, Naval Ravikant, Amanda Frances, Robin Sharma, and James Clear. Their books have massively impacted how I approach the business mindset; and I've learned to trust my own decision-making skills and intuition as an entrepreneur because of the teachings and wisdom of those who came before me. I'm a huge believer that a book is the best medium to transfer principles, stories and mindset, and inspire you to light a fire in your belly to take action and build that business of yours. That is why I'm writing this book and have devoted nearly four years doing so, in the hope that it serves your business journey.

So, let's start making those moves. Effortlessness is a myth. You have to put in the work to reap the results.

Chapter 1

My Wealthy Moves

If a young woman from a small town in India can build a million-dollar company, what makes you think you can't? A million dollars is life-changing. This amount is not small, at least in 2025. It could solve most of your money problems, allowing you to live a pretty comfortable life. Until it runs out. What then? How are you going to make the next million?

But before I answer that question, I want you to know one thing—your desire to make more money is valid. The universe has supported that desire in your heart, there is no reason to be ashamed or let anyone else make you feel ashamed because of your big, scary, life-changing goals.

Now, if you don't have crazy luxurious needs, you can live a pretty comfortable life. Your first million dollars gives you the opportunity to trust yourself, it gives you the possibility of multiplying it, and creating more impact. Anyone can create a successful profitable business, if that is what they desire. I meet a lot of clients who are very driven and ambitious. They want to go on luxurious vacations, send their kids to private schools, and live in the best neighbourhoods. These are all legitimate goals.

I've also met people in my client base who are not as driven to hit a million dollars but they want to be financially independent, and be financially free as well, so that they can spend more time with their families, or make enough money to travel the world full-time. What's a good number for that, you ask? $10,000 per month will allow anyone to live a simple and relaxed life, unburdened by the grind the rest of the world puts itself through.

Why should you believe a word of what I'm saying? I'm not perfect or great at business or insanely smart or anything. I'm just a girl from a small city in Gujarat, India, who took out an education loan to pay for her bachelor's degree in software engineering. Who wasn't born with a silver spoon in her mouth, who is not special or extra smart or a genius. I can only offer you one reason: I am a self-made millionaire. I started and built a million-dollar business from scratch without any network or venture funding or any connections.

And I'm just getting started.

I started my journey by offering marketing services such as Facebook Ads, Search Engine Optimizations and Sales Funnels to businesses across the world. This was the freelancing stage of my business. Three years later, I wanted to build leverage and stop trading time for money, so I transitioned to business coaching. Currently, our coaching programs, digital products and masterminds are the main revenue streams in the business. Through these, we train, mentor and coach our clients on skills such as Social Media Marketing, Meta Ads, Lead Generation, Sales Generation and Leveraging Digital Coaching Offers for their businesses.

I also take up private consulting clients for businesses that are in the 7-8-9 figure revenue range. I produce free content across all social media channels on a daily basis and send them to our 30,000 email subscribers. As I write this, I've run my businesses based out of India, Singapore, and presently, Dubai.

I am where I am, only because of believing it in my bones—that I and I alone am responsible for my wealthy moves, my success and my life.

***

I can't tell you the story about making money without mentioning how daunting it is. There were so many times when I had wanted to quit. More times than I can count. I even stalled writing this book, even as I was writing it, on a number of occasions before it saw the light of day. I've faced negativity, trolls, haters, hateful people, demeaning people, people who tried to tear me down and more.

I've made a lot of money, and then I've struggled with that. I've made very little money, then I've struggled to pay my bills and my team. I've had to borrow money sometimes to make payroll, or invest in a mentor or a course to keep working on my business goals. I've lost my health multiple times, and there have been some very embarrassing times where my body felt weak and my mind wary. I've debated my own role in relationships with my partners, parents, relatives and friends.

And truly, it is a journey. There's not a single person in the world who has got it all figured out. Even though social media will tell you otherwise. Whatever your circumstance, you are leading yourself. You have always led yourself—whether negatively or positively.

YOU are the magic.

YOU can make moves that can change your and your next generation's life.

So, let's stop blaming life, the universe, the creator, or other people for things that happen to you. While shit happens to us all sometimes, for no fault of our own, we can still lead ourselves through that.

Unlearning and Learning about Money Mindset

I had plenty of opportunities to view myself as a middle-class woman and stay in that mentality all through my life. But I knew that was no way for me to reach my true potential.

That being said, I definitely have a lot of privilege. I was born without any disability. I grew up in a stable home environment. I had a loving childhood and was blessed with a considerably good life and upbringing, where my parents spent a lot of time, energy and effort on my education and hobbies.

It was only at school that I began to notice how different things could be. Some of my classmates were allowed to have their own vehicles to commute, while I was still riding my bicycle to school. At university, there were classmates whose parents gave them hefty pocket money and were ready to fund their postgraduate education in the US or in Europe, while I had been forced to take out a student loan for my undergraduate degree. I'm not complaining though, all these life experiences made me scrappy, a useful trait if you want to be a CEO.

At present, I am in a position to enjoy my life, thanks to the moves I made from college till now. I've taught these tactics to my clients, and they have been creating wealth for themselves as well. Seeing them provide a better life for their family, purchasing their dream homes, buying their favourite car, traveling the world while working on their “little” side-hustle that have turned into full-fledged six and seven-figure brands is heartwarming.

It’s not all glitz and glamour, though. There are specific moves which helped my clients and me get here. And instead of gatekeeping, I want to share them with you:

Not letting my school or college grades define my job prospects.

Learning how to land high-end clientele for my freelancing services after quitting my job.

Learning how to leverage my story, skills, frameworks into a coaching program that scaled my business.

Learning to build a personal brand.

Money mindset for building and scaling a seven-figure brand.

Having multiple investments in real estate, in SAAS companies and public stock markets that grow month over month.

If learning and executing all this is important to you, you will enjoy this book.

Homework

Let's dig deep. Get yourself a journal and freely write about which wealthy moves are getting you excited right now.

Is it making more money so you can live in a better neighbourhood?

Is it attracting more wealth so you can take yourself on vacations while living in the best resorts?

Is it so you can send your kids to the best private schools and colleges in the world?

Is it so you can leave the world a better place than you found it?

Is it that you've gone through trauma, and hopelessness and pain and would like to help others through it?

I want you to be genuinely honest with yourself. Journal below for yourself—I call it the 'North Star Exercise'. Your *why* is important when the ride gets tough:

What do you desire from the bottom of your heart?

What keeps you going when nothing is going your way?

If you could have anything at all, with no limits, what would it be? Make your dreams as detailed as possible.

Where do you want to live, what do you want to do each day?

List down the reasons or the "why" behind all these dreams. Do it from a place of no-judgment, no-guilt zone.

What is the financial goal you want to achieve in the next year, next three years, next 10 years?

Lastly, list down the thoughts and feelings about what is stopping you from achieving these dreams.

Chapter 2

Failure Is Feedback

I had been at the top of my class all through middle school and high school. When I got into a decent college, one with a good reputation, all I could think of was "Freedom! Finally!" In my first semester, I was in a rebellious frame of mind, already feeling disinterested in the four years of coding, algorithms, algebra and data structures that were looming ahead of me.

So, I did everything except study. I went for basketball try-outs, dance club try-outs, spent hours in the library reading books, and skipped lectures. In fact, I think I skipped more lectures than I ever attended.

We can all see where this is going.

I didn't fail my courses during my first semester. But I might as well have. I think it was just a little bit of luck that I managed to get a passing grade. But they were the lowest grades I've ever scored. I got 4.7 out of 10. I'd always scored in the 80s and 90s in my school. Needless to say, my parents were upset. Their prodigiously talented daughter, the always-A-student, was now almost failing. It's important to note that the college I attended would rusticate students who scored below 4.0. I had just barely managed to survive. I felt so humiliated. I had struggled to succeed in a new environment where my past achievements were unknown.

I respect my father a lot. He has always encouraged excellence in every field, especially academics. I don't recall exactly what he said, but I know he didn't scold me that much. Which was weird, was he finally accepting me as an adult? Was he trying to tell me, that *"You reap what you sow, Roota."* And the days of my parents pushing me, getting me back on track were over. It was time to own up to my actions, and face the consequences, as an adult!

Looking back, I believe I was coasting through life at that point, and the high-pressure during the 11th and 12th grade had left me feeling burnt out. I faced difficulties with subjects like algebra and algorithms. I remember participating in group projects, but often taking a backseat and being more of a silent observer than a contributor. I struggled with laboratory work and coding projects as well, missing tutorials and lectures due to laziness or a lack of motivation. I still think of my college years as a failure because I feel like I had so much potential and I wasted it all away. I was jealous of the toppers, of people who were able to participate in the extracurricular clubs, while maintaining their grades.

I was unable to do any extracurriculars because I had to bring my grades back up.

I had brought all this upon myself because I didn't have a goal, I didn't have any motivation, I didn't have a clear path of what I wanted. This experience turned into a lesson that has really stuck with me, all through these years.

I felt extremely disappointed in myself. I vowed to redeem my grades and my self-respect before I graduated. In my second year of college, I studied hard and applied to hundreds of internships. I pushed through, even in subjects I didn't particularly like. Slowly but surely, I transitioned from being a passive participant in group projects to leading them, presenting, impressing my professors, and striving for higher grades.

I used job sites, internships sites, manually found email addresses of professors at renowned national institutions and wrote hundreds of personalized emails, asking them to hire me for an internship. Because I was hungry, I had no ego or shyness that stopped me from reaching out to professors who taught at different branches of the Indian Institute of Technology (IIT), even though my grades were still not top notch. I thought the worst thing they're going to do is say 'No' or not reply. I did get some positive replies even though I didn't land any internship at any of the IITs. Which was fine. It didn't kill my spirit.

However, one of the hundreds of companies I had applied to for internships replied and asked me to come to Ahmedabad, for an interview. This was an educational startup and they were hosting summer camps for kids in the eighth and ninth grades. I wasn't qualified to teach kids at all. But what did I have to lose, right?

The internship was for the position of a Teaching Assistant, alongside a Cryptography professor who would be teaching eighth-grade students the basics of Cryptography. Cryptography is the process of hiding or coding information so that only the person a message was intended for can read it. This is essentially used to secure information in banks, payment gateways, securing WhatsApp messages and more. I was studying the subject in college, and I wasn't even the top student in the course, but I had applied anyway.

I remember wearing a crisp white shirt and riding my scooter for two hours in the heat to reach the interview. I was desperate. I really wanted to turn my bad grades and broken self-confidence around. I was determined to do everything in my power to make something of myself. I don't recall doing anything outstanding during the interview, so I didn't really fancy my chances.

A couple days later, I received an email informing me that I had been accepted. I squealed with joy as I called my parents. The internship, which included boarding and food, was located at the big Infosys campus in the lovely city of Mysore in South India; and this stipend was the first real money I ever earned in my career.

I met incredible professors from all around the world, and my professor was incredibly patient and kind with me. I made such wonderful memories with friends during those three weeks. But most importantly, the internship gave me a bit of confidence. I wasn't the piece of crap I thought I was, and I had created this opportunity for myself, which meant that I could try and do it again.

Take the chance, you truly lose nothing.
If I was to give you any advice, don't be afraid to fail. I know you might have heard this before.
But the reason you don't take a chance on something new is because you're afraid of what people will think when you fail.
Let me tell you, no one is thinking about you.
No one cares.
They are all worried and thinking about themselves.

As the famous evangelist and author Norman Vincent Peale said, *"Shoot for the moon. Even if you miss, you'll land among the stars."*

This is what life is all about—overcoming burn out,

overwhelm and pushing yourself even though you stumble along the way.

***

Trigger Warning: Suicide.

There were some moments of despair too. A fellow student from our batch took their own life after being expelled from college because of low grades. I hadn't thought about this memory for years until my recent visit to my college. It reminded me of how we often feel that academic grades, getting into top colleges, or securing a good job placement defines our worth as humans. This incident made me realize that it's easy to think that failure in these areas means we've failed as individuals. I also think of times during my 12th board exams where I felt frustrated, and didn't want to be in this world anymore. I want to emphasize and let you know that if you too were a 17-year-old or a 25-year-old who felt like a failure, you're not alone.

The challenges I faced during college that seemed so BIG at the time have proven to be minor in the grand scheme of things, and a very small part of a long and fulfilling life. You have multiple opportunities ahead. If something isn't your passion or is draining your energy, it's okay to make a change. Don't subject your loved ones or your future self to such drastic actions.

Life is full of possibilities—one can find their great

love, travel to new places, create memories, build relationships, have a successful career, and develop self-confidence. It's important not to take yourself too seriously and to face life's ups and downs with resilience.

When your stock is down, you'll find your real friends.
When your stock is down, you build character.
When your stock is down, you learn to truly enjoy the highs of life and value them.

I encourage you to reach out to friends, family, or suicide support hotlines. Remember that the world needs you, and whatever challenges you're facing now, you have the strength to overcome them. Believe in yourself and take a step toward an enriched future. You've got this; you are stronger than you think. I am rooting for you.

Life is a Wave Form

My experiences have taught me that life is a wave form. Whenever there's an up, there's always a down. Then comes another "up", and so on. My failures and feedback in college taught me that it's okay to not always be on top. I learnt that you have to keep proving yourself to the world. No one cares what your school grades were, when you join college, and not many will care about college grades when you enter the workforce. The scoreboard is wiped clean, and you need to prove yourself to the world again. "You are only as good as your last sale"—I heard a real estate agent say this on

TV, and it has been stuck in my mind ever since.

Grades Don't Matter *That* Much

The thing you need to learn is, if you had bad grades in school/college, that doesn't mean you won't be successful in your career or business. Sure, it's difficult to get jobs or get into a higher-level college if your grades are bad. But you can either make excuses and let it stop you, or you push ahead.

I landed a job at a major consulting firm during my college placements, which paid quite well. But then, I managed to clear the interview for the higher-paying software startup where I ended up working for two and a half years. So, I graduated with two job offers despite my grades. You see, not everything is messed up when you have bad grades. If you truly work hard, you can turn the scoreboard in your favour. And that's what matters.

The game is only lost when you stop trying. You get the final say on the scoreboard of your life. No one else.

Today, my company has helped so many young people land internships, high-paying freelancing gigs and marketing jobs with our skills programs. Empowering 20-year-olds with an alternate career choice and passion has been one of the best rewards about running an online education company.

I loved college—the friends, the network and the memories will stay with me forever. I love traditional education systems, in the sense that it teaches you discipline, social skills and meeting awesome people. But if you want to thrive in today's digital economy, you need to do more. You have to invest in learning real-life skills. Maybe you're into stock investing, or maybe learning art really drives your fancy, or maybe you want to be a professional chef, or maybe you want to learn sales, marketing and money mindset from me. Whatever your priorities are, find an online course or a physical conference that can help you get there.

Find a mentor that has done what you want to do, and soak everything from them.

In one of his talks, Naval Ravikant, the founder of Angellist, and a modern-day philosopher said, "The future will be almost all startups". I'm a huge fan of his book, *The Almanack of Naval Ravikant*, and have read it, from cover to cover, many times. His views on modern philosophy and generating wealth by building leverage has impacted me a lot. I agree with him, too. Everyone will be a contractor for hire in the next 10-50 years. Rather than applying for jobs, you'll be applying for gigs. You can decide your schedule. You can take three weeks off as you desire. You can work when you want, where you want.

And for that, you need to build practical skills that work in the real world, and I'm here to show you how.

Know When to Move On

My job is not to convince you whether working at a job is the right decision for you. You know that best.

My corporate journey didn't start off too shabbily. The first two years of my job were awesome. I had been brought up in a home where money was always tight. My parents believed in investing in my education, extracurriculars and my growth. Our family was prudent when it came to spending.

Growing up, all I wanted was financial freedom. I wanted to be able to buy what I wanted and go travel whenever I wanted, that's it. While working at my corporate job, I was able to buy what I wanted and travel to a bunch of places and stay in nice hotels. It was all fun for about two years. But then, the realization hit me. Is this *all* there is to life?

Working most weekends, working for more than 10-12 hours on weekdays, taking a couple of vacations a year, online shopping when I was stressed and overworked, and always working hard to build someone else's dream. At 23, after spending two-and-a-half-years in the corporate world, I was creatively unfulfilled. I couldn't dream of spending my life in that world till I reached 60 and was ready to retire.

When money and material things are your sole motivation in life, it gets old pretty fast.

That is not something which motivates you for long, and soon, you start to see the sacrifices you made to achieve all this leads to more stress, your health is affected majorly, and you have no real freedom. All I was doing was working, eating junk, never exercising and partying with friends in my free time. I was diagnosed with Polycystic Ovary Syndrome (PCOS) during that time which led to me putting on weight and suffering from terrible face acne.

Now, most of this had nothing to do with the job itself. People with corporate jobs can workout, eat healthy and take better care of themselves. But the stress and unhappiness about a lot of job-related things were real. And because I was unhappy, I resorted to all the unhealthy activities for instant gratification. I don't even recognize that person now. The person who abused her body, because she was extremely unhappy at work. All this had been going on for a while, but this still wasn't the straw that broke the camel's back. All the unhappiness was affecting my work which led to me not receiving the yearly appraisal I wanted. All of my peers and colleagues in the office got a hefty raise—not me, even though I was still working long hours and weekends.

I was extremely embarrassed and ashamed. I felt like a failure again, just like I did after the first year in college. I battled with my self-worth for months, crying to my family and saying that this is not where I belong. By the time my tears dried, I knew one thing for certain: if my efforts were not valued, then I'd rather walk away. If I was spending this much time building someone else's dream, sacrificing my mental and physical health, I'd rather do this for myself. If I really wanted more freedom for my life, be it location-based, time-based, income-based, I had to start my own business.

I Quit My High-paying Job as a Software Developer at 23

Making the decision to quit my high-paying job was not easy. My head was filled with doubts about how I would pay my bills. I had saved up some money to ensure I had enough runway for a couple of months, close to a year, but that was it.

But what would happen if I burnt through my savings, and 12 months later didn't have anything to show for it? My friends and family didn't understand what I wanted to do.

My parents were against my decision to quit my job. I don't blame them. Who in their right mind resigns from a nice cushy job at the beginning of their career? But when you're making big moves in your life, your loved ones will rarely understand. This is completely normal, and it doesn't mean that you need to retrace your steps. The passion, pain and fire burning within you is so big, no one around you understands it. I want you to know that you don't need anyone's approval or permission to take accountability of your own life and wealthy moves.

Now logically, their worry for me made complete sense. *Why was I giving up so soon?* They worried for me, tried to explain to me that life is long and that you can quit later, that this is youthful arrogance. But to me, those 30 months were enough for this lifetime. My boss at the time really tried talking me into continuing the job, bless his heart. But I don't think *anything, anyone or any amount of money* would've stopped me then. Eventually, I convinced my parents to let me quit.

I was nervous.

The nagging doubts in my mind didn't go away. It's absolutely scary to jump into the unknown. But even more so when you don't have a clue about what you're going to do to pay your bills. I wasn't sure this was a smart move. What if nothing worked and after a year, I needed to come back and get a job, but no one would hire me because I spent a year "failing" to be my own boss?

I had a minor inkling that I could maybe learn social media and something could come out of it. This was back in 2015, so monetizing on social media wasn't as popular as it is today. While working at my job, I was working on a travel blog on the side. I had a few thousand followers, and about 10 blog posts on my WordPress blog. I was making exactly $0.00 from it. In 2016 too, just like now, there was no dearth of travel bloggers and standing out was extremely difficult, let alone making a decent income out of it. I didn't want to create content for brands who would pay pennies or create content for free or barter in the hope of generating any income from my blog.

To be honest, I wanted to make enough money to not just be comfortable and pay my bills, but to travel to new places while working; to make sure I took my parents on their first international vacation and pampered them; to ensure I could hire people to help me and contribute to their career; to secure a good future for my family after I got married.

And most importantly, I didn't want to depend on my father or my future partner for completing all my hopes and dreams. I wanted to be fully self-dependent. And this fire, to do exactly this, made me dive into the unknown even though I was scared shitless.

When is the Right Time to Quit Your Job?

I wanted to be smart about it. I had saved up for nearly a year before I decided to take the leap. I had no dependents or responsibilities and I was grateful for that. There was my college education loan which I had already paid off while working. So I was debt-free, which helped a lot as well.

If you have dependents or debts or responsibilities, jot them down and divide them into monthly payments. If you feel like having two years of living expenses saved up would make you feel at peace, make a plan today on how you are going to do that. With everything included, you should have at least a year's worth of expenses and payments saved up. The more the better, of course.

A Word of Encouragement

Sometimes we take ourselves so seriously, and overthink every decision. Dinosaurs, the biggest creatures the planet has seen, disappeared from Earth in the blink of an eye. We have countless stars in the galaxies, and we are tiny specks within it. People won't remember our mistakes and failures after we die; people won't remember us a week after our funeral. It's time to be braver with our pursuits while we're alive. Sometimes, you have to let the fire overpower your fears, and awesome things are waiting to happen. Your dreams have already come true in the spiritual world, you just have to *will* them to be true in the physical world.

Homework: Visualize and Journal

What do you wish you could forgive yourself for?

What are the moments in your life when you felt like a failure in the past?

Reframe each of those failures and feedback. What would you say to yourself about each of those experiences?

Failure builds character.

Journal about the things you're grateful for that made you build a strong character and grow resilience.

Chapter 3

Your First Six Figures is a Bitch, But You Gotta Do It

"It's a bitch, but you gotta do it. I don't care what you have to do—if it means walking everywhere and not eating anything that wasn't purchased with a coupon, find a way to get your hands on $100,000," said Charlie Munger, Warren Buffet's business partner. He was talking about how getting to your first $100,000 is critical. That first chunk of real big money gives you the confidence and skills to then do it multiple times over and become a millionaire. It all starts with landing your first client to sell your services to.

How I Landed My First Client

After I quit my job, I felt skill-less and to be honest, I was starting from scratch. I had no marketable skills, no connections to the marketing world, no MBA degree or higher education, no family connections, no funding—nothing.

My only skill was coding in Java, and troubleshooting server issues; skills I didn't want to keep using to freelance anymore as they didn't fulfill me creatively. In addition to that, I was working on my travel blog, "The Purple Backpack", on the side, and that was making me no money at all. But it taught me the skill of writing. I've written countless ad copies, marketing emails, sales pages, built educational presentations, scripted videos—and I'm in the process of writing this book. That blog was the start to my writing journey.

During that time, I realized I didn't know how to market my travel blog. I decided to run a few Meta (Facebook) Ads back then, even though I barely knew what I was doing. I genuinely thought I was wasting a few thousand rupees, and making a dent in my already-declining savings.

In spite of my nervousness, I decided to go ahead. I was a bit gutsy and thought what's the worst that could happen, I would lose some money but at least I would make progress. I believe that bias towards action has served me well. People stay in their head for too long, and they collect zero data. But when you spend money, run ads, invest in a mentor—you get data first. And then you make better decisions based on data.

I ran a few ads, spent close to 10,000 INR, and got a few leads for my travel-planning services. I received three applications from people looking for travel planning services. Since I'd been to a few countries, I thought I could make a side-hustle income by planning itineraries and travel for some folks. An acquaintance from my job reached out to me to plan their next trip, so I reckon that the ads got a return on investment (ROI) indirectly already. Nothing much happened out of those applications that came in from the ads though.

However, the good thing was that I had data. The screenshots from my ads manager of the ads I had run, how much I had spent, how many leads I got, the ad creatives I used, the ad copy I wrote. I used these exact ad campaigns and lead screenshots to land my first paid USA-based client.

My last day of the job was August 30, 2016. I got my first client on October 30.

I remember it very well because it was also the day of Diwali. My parents had come to visit me where I was staying in a shared apartment with two other people in Gurgaon. We were standing out on the balcony of my apartment, looking at the firecrackers and lanterns. When the Gmail app on my phone buzzed, and the client with whom I had my first discovery all, said YES to my ads proposal.

I got this client from a Facebook group full of

entrepreneurs. This particular client had put up a post wanting to hire someone for Facebook Ads for their PR firm. When I chanced upon this post, it already had hundreds of comments from people much more experienced than me.

If you didn't know by now, everyone starts small. Don't wait till someone knocks on your door and hands you a job. Surprise, it's never going to happen. People care about their own dreams, not about your dreams. You have got to go out there and make it happen for yourself. I did think to myself: *"I don't have enough experience with ads"*, or *"There are hundreds of experienced people, who will even hire me"*, or *"I suck at ads, why would she hire me"* ...but I applied anyway and landed the gig.

This client had also paid the deposit for $70, the first installment of our project. It was a $280 proposal for a month. Not life-changing money by any means, but it was a start. I told my parents at that moment, and their faces lit up with happiness. I could also sense a bit of pride in their eyes.

All those tough conversations months ago about quitting the job didn't matter now. Because even though it was only one client, and it was a tiny amount, it was the start of so much more. I worked very hard to get this client's results. I created a few ad campaigns, managed them daily, sent weekly reports to the client, wrote copies and designed creatives, even though I wasn't getting paid a lot.

I was so happy because I had figured out how to monetize my new skills.

Sadly, the client didn't renew the contract after a month, because their business wasn't ready for ads then. It was a bit of a bummer to lose my first client after only a month. But they were so happy with my service and the leads I got them, that they wrote me an awesome testimonial. And I used that testimonial and the ad campaign screenshots to land another client.

This time for $660 per month!

I *doubled* my prices with the next Australia based client who wanted me to run ads for their interior designing offers.

Don't have the skills? *Get them!*
Don't have any client projects or case study? *Get them by doing the work on yourself as a case study.*
Don't have a big following? *Work every day to build it.*
No one is going to knock your door and hand over the skills, your first client, and the confidence to deliver the client results to you. *You have to make the moves.*

I get it, imposter syndrome is a thing. But doing the work is the only thing that will give you confidence, nothing else. No number of motivational books, videos or speakers will give you confidence. You will give yourself the confidence when you actually go out, get your hands dirty and do it.

How to Get Your First or Next Client

Getting your first few clients in your one-person business is crucial. Before you even think about hiring a team or running advertising or think about any other distractions.

I've employed a lot of methods to get clients. Some creative, some weird; some worked, some massively failed. There were numerous times when I took a flight, economy class, for a 24-hour journey, one way, to attend conferences in the United States. Where I was the only Indian person who had flown thousands of kilometers to be there to grow my own company. I've done this multiple times in the early years of my company. I didn't know anyone at those conferences, I didn't have any friends in America yet, and as a vegetarian, I wasn't used to American food—let's just say that it was daunting. I wasn't used to the business culture in the world, outside of India. I learnt it all on the go and I figured it out because I was hungry to learn. I learned from incredible entrepreneurs like Alex and Leila Hormozi, Russell Brunson, Sam Ovens and so many other entrepreneurs.

It was also wildly freeing at the time, to travel, learn and work on my company and make friends and do something. I haven't attended a conference in years, now I tend to trust my gut as a CEO so much more. But I firmly believe that my hustle at the time was needed and paid me in skills and connections much more than if I had stayed in my comfort zone. Failure was just not an option for me. I did everything in my power to learn everything I could by attending conferences, and learning from mentors and learning from people who were a few steps ahead of me in business and marketing.

Go out and meet people.
Travel to new cities and countries and make friends.
Go attend conferences and masterminds and retreats.
Go where your favourite author/thinker is speaking and learn from them.
Go where it's uncomfortable even though you're scared. You won't die, I promise you and you'll have learnt something new.
Go where your favourite CEOs and tech founders congregate and ask them questions.
Go where you'll be intellectually challenged and question everything you've ever known.

In Business, Testimonials Are Your Life-blood

If you're in a service-based business, testimonials and reviews are so important!

I've hired so many people for various services, and it's shocking to me how so many freelancers after years of experience have zero testimonials. It's a major deterrent for me in hiring them.

If you have worked for someone to fulfill their project, you deserve a testimonial. Unless you pissed them off majorly and did not do a fine job, they will be happy to give you a testimonial. A video testimonial is the best, you can use the script below to request a testimonial:

"Hey John/Jane, it's been a real pleasure working with you over the past few months. As you know, I'm a freelancer and client reviews are the best things that help me grow my business. Whenever you have a moment, would you mind recording a short video talking about your honest experience working with me? You can choose to include these three things: how was your business before you met me as compared to how it is now; what was the best part about working with me; and if you can add actual sales/lead numbers we've achieved together—that would just be the cherry on the cake. Thank you so much."

Make changes to the script based on your niche, offer and personality, so it doesn't sound weird when you use my words. But essentially, this is what we want to convey.

I've never met a client who refused a video testimonial to me—*you just have to ask.*

There was a time in business where I'd taken a couple months off to get married. As a one-person business without a team or a predictable sales system set up at the time, I was experiencing a long dry period in business. There had been no revenue for months, and I felt like I was starting from scratch yet again. I was in deep despair—did taking time off affect my business momentum? What if I couldn't get to my previous revenue levels? Was this the end of my business? Will I have to go back to that job I had quit just three short years ago?

Somehow, I generated a fuel of energy within myself to keep going; I had to work towards the future despite these unhelpful thoughts. My gratitude practice saved my business yet again.

I started implementing new things by treating my business as its own marketing case study; I tried new stuff on Instagram, and created a framework that worked well for me to grow my following and get leads for my business. Luckily, my client outreach efforts helped me land a done-for-you client. A done-for-you client is where you offer them end-to-end marketing services and do the execution for them. This is different from a coaching client: when you provide guidance and mentorship but they do the execution themselves.

I treat my own business as a massive experimentation machine and that's how I've been able to get out of the slump. Why can't I utilize the same tactics I use for my client and get the same, if not better results?

I asked one of my clients for a video testimonial, and to my surprise, they obliged. They called me a 'money-making genius' in their video—an overstatement, I feel, but they shared some real numbers of how my services and framework benefitted them in their business. That video testimonial, years later, continues to build trust and adds to the social proof we have in our business. I shared this testimonial everywhere on my social media. I was then able to land a second done-for-you client, and a third consulting client for the same framework! All of a sudden, I went from zero momentum and zero clients, to a roster full of high-end clients because I kept going and I wasn't shy to ask for testimonials.

To this day, nine years later in business, our testimonials still bring in the most business, when used strategically. You can make promises all day long, about how cool and amazing your offers are. But testimonials actually prove that you're not tooting your own horn. Getting others to say your offers are as amazing as you say they are goes a long way. But every entrepreneur must ensure one thing—the praise must be rooted in honesty and authenticity. Otherwise, you are asking a client to lie on your behalf, and any house of cards built on those claims tends to collapse on itself, sooner than later.

Double Your Rates with Each Client

I started a habit of doubling my rates with every client at the start of my freelance career. Some people will call that crazy but I never wanted to be comfortable charging a specific amount, because as I grew my skills, I reckoned that I deserved to get paid more.

Pricing is relative.

What may be expensive for some, may not be for others. And if you charge low, clients will think twice about hiring you. Because they're not just investing their money in you, they are also investing their time and energy. If they don't think you're worth it, why would they take a chance on you? The best way to let a client know you're not worth it is by charging too low. They think, if you don't value your services enough to charge your worth, why should I? And bam! You lost the client.

I doubled my price after every client because I wanted to keep growing, leveling up my skills and charging my worth accordingly. It forced me to not stay too much within my comfort zone, and to always come up with new ways to over-deliver to my clients. Because of this, in my third month of freelancing, I hit my first-ever $5,000 month, which was almost as close to the monthly salary I earned at my previous job.

Become Obsessed with One Skill

I don't recommend becoming a jack of all trades—become obsessed with mastering one skill.

For me, it was Facebook Ads. This skill has served me well over the years, and has been the backbone of my marketing business. I got 1:1 done-for-you clients and consulting for that; and I taught my coaching clients how to leverage their ad skills to cross six and seven figure marks in their business.

I recommend learning the basics of ads creation and scaling yourself up. Delegate ads management only if you are short on time. Learning advertising skills made sure I was never reliant on expensive ad agencies for my business growth. Advertising teaches you to write better, to write persuasively, to create graphics and videos that stop the scroll and catch people's attention. My digital program 'Ads Simplified' is the best way to learn my most prized skill. Find more information on my website *www.learnwithroota.com*.

Build Continuity Offers to Keep Hitting Consistent $10,000 months

Having retainer clients is key for generating a consistent income. It's possible to make $10,000 in a single month, but for steady earnings, you need retainer clients rather than just one-off projects.

Longer retainer contracts are even better. Just be careful not to undercharge, especially if you're committing to a long-term deal. Three-month retainers are a good start, and some people even secure six-month-long or yearly contracts. You can sign clients with a minimum three-month requirement. I highly recommend this if you're selling social media, marketing, launch and business development services.

Remember, transformation isn't achieved overnight.

About 90 days is the perfect time to achieve a big milestone in their business. If you over-promise the result you can achieve for them in 30 days, they are definitely not going to renew the contract and they'll leave with a bad experience because you couldn't manage their expectations better.

I've learned that building and maintaining strong relationships with my clients is absolutely crucial. I always try to go the extra mile for them. For instance, when one of my clients landed a big contract, I sent them a handwritten card congratulating them, along with a bouquet of flowers.

Another time, I remembered a client mentioning their love for a specific type of chocolate, so I surprised them with a box on the day of their company's anniversary. Just last week, I spent an extra hour on a call with a client who was struggling with a personal issue, even though it wasn't strictly business-related. I focus on giving them not just great service, but a great experience overall.

It's amazing how this approach pays off. I've found that when I genuinely care for my clients, the money and retainers tend to follow naturally. My longest-standing client has been with me for five years now, all because I prioritized our relationship from day one.

Even with my mastermind, we have the annual continuity offer where clients choose to renew for a second and third year within our program. We have built a community where clients find their "second home" as they want to keep being in the energy of the mastermind. It truly warms my heart that we have clients who decide to stay under my mentorship for years. Business wise, this is important to grow the Lifetime Value (LTV) of a customer instead of constantly searching for new clients.

Start Selling VIP Days

A pivotal moment in my freelancing journey was landing a $1,500 client for a two-hour consultation about sales funnels and ads.

My husband was working in the other room, I raced over and told him when that invoice was settled. It brought immense joy and pride that despite all the setbacks, trials and tribulations, there were some serious wins to be proud of. It had been a long journey, from initially charging $280 per month, and now landing a $1,500 client for just a two-hour consultation. It felt incredible.

There were countless days of self-doubt and self-pity. I wondered if freelancing was for me or not. I remembered it was about 18 months into the journey, when I wanted to quit so bad. I was tired of bad clients sucking up all my energy, tired of the income rollercoasters and unsustainable income, tired of feeling like a failure in this business I had started. So I had to come up with a different strategy, one that would work in the long term.

First, I love starting with a quick 30-minute discovery call. It's my chance to get to know potential clients and see if we click.

When it comes to pricing, I've learned not to undervalue myself. In the beginning, I started at $300 for a two-hour session. I then applied my double-your-price principle with every consulting client going forward. That's how I closed a $1,500 VIP Day client.

Once a client is on board and the invoice is paid, I dive deep into their world. I ask about their top three problems and get all the details. I request links to their website, funnels, and social media. I want to know everything about the offer they're launching and all their business data—leads, costs, conversion rates, you name it. I always remind myself that I'm not just selling my time—I'm offering a transformation! *An outcome!*

By gathering all this information upfront, I make sure I am prepared to knock their socks off during our consulting session. It makes me confident since I could spend my time wisely and complete my research, and plan a business development strategy before our consultation call.

I encourage you to start selling two-hour/four-hour-long VIP Consulting days on top of your services to make some extra cash, and nurture some leads which could turn into long-term client relationships as well.

Homework: Create a Game Plan and Start Executing

What action are you going to take starting today to get your first or next client?

Ask for a video testimonial from three clients you've worked with or three people who you have helped for free or charged very little.

Mastermind on how you are going to double your price with your next client.

Start creating an offer for your VIP Consulting Day. This works regardless of your niche.

Which continuity offer are you going to build in your business to hit consistency in sales?

Chapter 4

Business Lies You Should Stop Believing

In this digital age, we have access to a lot of resources and information. And that is why you need to learn discernment and not believe everything you hear or read online. In this chapter, I want to point out the bad advice you might have received that is keeping you stuck—and the lies you have been told about growing your business and landing premium clientele.

I have to admit that some of these lies kept me stagnant for a long time, longer than I'm proud to admit. My hope is for you to develop discernment and decision-making skills to filter the advice you receive smartly, and create your own principles to rely on for your business.

These are the lies I choose to relentlessly call bullshit on so you can break through to your next wealth milestone.

Lie: You Need to Charge Per Hour to Get Clients

In the eight years of my business, I have never charged hourly.

Even when I was a beginner, a freelancer making $0 per month, my rates were based on the project, the value, ROI, and the outcomes I was providing. If you go down the hourly pricing road, then you are charging your client a fee that is based on the amount of time it takes for you to complete the task.

Now all these years down the line, you are likely to have learned how to do the task faster, smarter, and in a way that is more valuable to your clients. So, if you're still charging by the hour, you are doing nothing but punishing yourself. You only have limited hours in a day, and you can only take up so many clients during the day. And that's why I don't recommend charging hourly—even if you're just starting out.

Lie: You Need to Get Clients from Freelancing Websites

I don't recommend getting gigs on freelancing sites like Fiverr, Upwork, and some others of this sort, because you are competing with thousands of other people solely based on their prices. Not your skills, not your expertise, just their low prices.

I have worked with over 4,000 entrepreneurs, freelancers, agency owners, consultants and coaches to know that you need to avoid working on platforms where people find the cheapest option to get the job done. If pricing is the only basis of hiring, then there will always be someone charging less than you. *You cannot win a price war!*

Lie: You Don't Deserve to Charge High-end Prices

I have seen my clients go from charging a few hundred dollars to sending multiple thousand-dollar proposals and closing these deals with confidence.

My clients range from 18-year-olds completing their college degrees and working on their freelance business on the side, to 45-year-old executives who have left their decades-long corporate career behind because of burnout—and everyone in between.

The first step to charging a high-ticket price is for you to believe that you can charge it. And that belief sometimes can take days, weeks, months or years to form. My hope for you is to shrink that timeline and drum up your confidence to get ready to charge a high-ticket price as soon as possible, and I hope this book will encourage you to do so!

At the start of your business, you will be motivated to charge the least and say yes to every client who enquires with you. This is exactly how waves of new freelancers and coaches get stuck in the cycle of charging low-tickets and are never able to break through to high-end prices. I recommend working with fewer clients and charging them well so that you are able to provide them with a better experience. It takes the same amount of effort to sell a high-ticket offer as it is to sell a low-ticket one, and only one can ensure that you will emerge happier.

You don't have to say yes to every client. You must filter clients from Day 1, and work with the clients who can pay you what you demand. When you are paid at the higher-end, you can then build the resources and profit margin to hire the right team members or part-time freelancers to deliver a better client experience—and have enough of a profit margin left for you so as not to feel like you are living paycheck to paycheck, or that you are always chasing after the next client.

Lie: You Need to Hustle to Make Your First Six-figures

I won't lie, you do have to work long hours and put in the sweat equity before you get some work-life balance going on. But that doesn't mean you can't have fun along the way.

My freelancing business allowed me tons of flexibility, so I could work from wherever I wanted. All I needed was a laptop and the Internet and I was good to go. In 2017, I attended a marketing conference in San Diego, while also keeping time aside to roam around sunny California, which I had always dreamed of doing.

At the conference, I met marketers and business owners from all around the world. It was a great place for networking, making friends and signing clients too. It was unbelievable to me that I was able to explore San Diego's incredible beaches, experience Hollywood, go to Universal Studios and ride in all the theme park rides by myself… all while working on my freelance business.

That time was truly a gift. I was able to be a free wild bird, go where the wind would take me. This is exactly why I quit my job. I couldn't just take off on a three-week trip to the US back when I was a corporate employee. They would have fired me as soon as I returned, no questions asked.

I couldn't rest my feet when I returned home from my US trip. I wanted more. The ability to work from anywhere was incredibly freeing. I was also making decent money, so I was already saving up for my next vacation. Or shall I say work-cation. So, for my birthday, I took another three-week-long solo trip across Southeast Asia. I visited Indonesia and Cambodia. I visited Angkor Wat, which is one of the wonders of the world, and it was so serene. I remember being extremely grateful, surrounded on all sides by ancient temples, but also enclosed by greenery, mountains and lakes. On my 24th birthday, I was all alone in the Gilli islands of Indonesia, enjoying the crystal blue waters. It was so crazy because only a year ago, I was unhappy, depressed and felt stuck in life working at my job. *A year can change so much in your life.*

My schedule was light and quite a lot of fun during that time: I used to do all my client calls in the morning, and then devote at least three-four hours to the client's project work during the morning, and the rest of the day was all mine. They were based in the US or UK, so the morning hours were perfect to connect with them.

I was free to do whatever I wanted to do that day—go scuba diving at one of the best dive sites in the world, laze around at the beach, go snorkeling, meet up new people and mingle, read a book while staring at the ocean, and write in my journal.

Lie: A Client Not Renewing Their Contract is Your Fault

I was working with a client, a long-term one, and I was charging them quite low. After a few months, when I sent them an email stating that I was going to increase my rates, there was a huge discussion that turned out to be a rather eye-opening experience for me.

During our conversation, I told them that I constantly invest in attending conferences and courses to level up, and the charges they were paying me were at the beginner level; now that my skills had improved since they had first hired my services, it was time to increase the price. But what came through was an emotional email: *"Only one of our campaigns is doing well. I'm hoping we can keep the same rates as we've been working together for a long time. The rest of the campaigns aren't doing well, and I'm starting to think it's my product. It might not be good enough."*

Sometimes we think it's all our fault if a client relationship doesn't go through. But our clients are all humans too, and they have their own issues and troubles that are stressing them out. They have doubts and fears just like anyone else. They are not above us and we're not below them.

It is a peer-to-peer relationship.

This just goes to show that business is tough for everyone. Because getting into business is all about trying, testing a thousand things, and maybe only a couple of them work, and some others don't. At that point, what do you do? You can close up shop or try another way to save the business. It's tough for clients and freelancers both, and I learnt that through this situation.

Lie: Brown People Can't Charge White People Prices

I feel somewhat vulnerable sharing this, but I think it is important.

There were times I used to feel embarrassed about my skin colour, accent, or simply the fact that I came from India. There is a great deal of baggage that citizens of formerly-colonized countries in the Global South carry, and I was no different. When I had the opportunity to present myself and my services to clients worldwide, I often underestimated myself. This was partly influenced by the way Indian people were portrayed in the media, in movies such as *Slumdog Millionaire* and characters in shows like *The Simpsons*. However, I came to realize that I was mistaken. It is important to embrace and take pride in your culture, background, and everything your parents have worked so hard to provide.

In my freelancing days, I've gone on sales calls with prospective clients who have been shocked after hearing my Meta ad services pricing. They couldn't believe I was charging as much as US service providers. Even when I had on-par results to show for myself. I invest in the best quality conferences, education and resources to keep my ads knowledge updated, I hire the right people to support my clients, and I had no shame in telling them that our services are no lesser just because I was based in India. There were prospects who respected that and became clients. There were others whose disapproval didn't matter to me and I had no interest in lowering my prices for them.

You are unique, and your skin tone, race, religion, history, and background make you who you are. Embrace it and be proud. If someone doesn't want to work with you based on those reasons, it is not the right partnership, and they are not the right client for you anyway. There are better clients out there, and there is no need to make time for bigots.

Never make yourself smaller to fit into other people's narrow minds.

Lie: Hitting $10,000 Months is Out of Reach For Me

Becoming a six-figure business owner is essentially you working towards making $10,000 months.

Experimenting in business has always served me well. You have to approach everything as an experiment. Start with a hypothesis, and complete the experiment, because in the end, you will either be proven wrong with data to improve, or you will succeed, and the rest will be history.

During one of these experiments, I was able to find a unique way of growing and attracting my ideal audience on Instagram. I started offering my Instagram services after using my own proprietary method of Instagram attraction and growth. I was so proud to come up with something that I could call my own.

And I charged high-end prices to my clients offering these services.

In August 2018, I hit $10,000 months with clients and

a few short months later, I executed my experiments with my Instagram strategy. This was such an important moment for me. It was the *one* goal I was dying to achieve when I started my freelancing journey, and it took me a full two years to be here. I couldn't believe how close I was to giving up only a few months ago, after my time-off for my wedding. It's true, when you feel like giving up, you don't know how close you are to success.

I'd come close to hitting $10,000 months a couple times before, but never was able to make a breakthrough. At the start of 2018, I'd almost hit that milestone but fell just short of the number. At the time, I had about four or five clients. One of them was a big client paying $2,500 a month, while the others were paying around $800 each. That month, I'd earned almost $9,000 and thought for sure that I was going to hit my first $10K month. When I quit my job in November 2016 and got my first client, reaching $10,000 a month was my main goal. After two years of hard work, I was thrilled to be so close.

But then, a client was slow in paying their invoice. I thought about asking them to process the payment faster but didn't want to seem pushy. Unfortunately, they didn't clear the invoice that month, so I ended up with just under $10,000. The next month, they ended up paying the invoice, and along with my other ongoing clients, I finally reached and even exceeded that coveted $10K/month goal for myself.

Homework: Journal It Out

What lies are you telling yourself that are keeping you stuck in making wealthy moves?

What lies are others telling you that are keeping you plateaued in business?

Which people, social media profiles and inputs are you going to remove from your life, so that you cut out the weeds and focus on your true potential?

Chapter 5

Build Leverage

"Earn with your mind, not your time," says author and investor Naval Ravikant in his bestselling book, *The Almanack of Naval Ravikant.*

Your first six figures are most likely achieved by trading time for money, by offering 1:1 consulting services or 1:1 coaching to clients. After your first six figures, it's time to build leverage. If you don't, you'll likely burn out and feel plateaued in business.

Document Your Journey to Six Figures

In my second year of business, I started showing up on videos, doing Instagram lives, and started building my audience by sharing content online.

Offer something of value first, before asking your audience for something in return.

I started my own Facebook group and used it to share my learning and my expertise. I did so with authority, and by that, I mean I was simply five steps ahead of my audience. I believed that what I was sharing was valuable, even though I was a young entrepreneur. Even though there were existing Facebook groups owned by people more well known and more successful than me, I didn't let that stop me. I began sharing what I was doing, outlined my data with my marketing experiments, and essentially documented my day-to-day workflows.

My Facebook group comprised of 400 people at the time, so I built up the audience from scratch. No advertisements, no collaborations, just pure organic outreach and content. Whoever you see flaunting millions of followers today, started with a single follower. *You got this.* You're not unique or weird in this journey. Your first few content pieces will feel cringey. Be ready to suck for a long time, to finally *get good* at your craft.

This initiative boosted my client acquisition and retention rate too, because when people see you show up, be confident, and teach your favourite topics, it makes your social proof go up. I also got four people to join my first-ever coaching program at $1,000 each, a crazy amount to come from a small Facebook group. The program taught them how they could build a freelance marketing business for themselves and market their own businesses better. This was an incredibly important exercise because I finally learnt to leverage my time better with 1: many offers rather than burning myself out selling 1:1 offers only.

I was only a few steps ahead of these program students, I was not a millionaire or anything by that point. But the important thing was that they wanted to learn from me, because they trusted me. And I knew more than them, which is what mattered.

I worked hard on delivering results to my program students, because even though I had only four people sign up for my program, they deserved my complete attention.

I was still working with 1:1 clients at this point, so I had two sources of revenue. I was working with high-ticket clients charging anywhere from $3,000-$5,000 per month per client for my services. I was contributing to their launches and income in an impactful way. In turn, they were able to have six-figure launches because of our marketing and advertising implementation, ultimately getting them to post a seven-figure annual revenue.

Your Shift from 1:1 Services to 1: Many Programs

At that time, I had an epiphany, if I could ensure these kinds of results for my clients, what was stopping me from doing this for myself?

I thought long and hard about not working with clients. Please note, this wasn't easy. Client revenue was still significant and it was still paying for my team, the various software and advertising expenses. My course was not that huge yet.

But I badly wanted to focus on my own business. *To focus relentlessly on growing my own business, instead of anyone else's anymore.* The client revenue didn't make sense for the time or energy I was putting into it, not to mention the added stress. If I could put that focus into my own business and products, I could make it much bigger and help more people along the way. I had worked with clients for three years, and had a wealth of experience now. I wanted to use that to scale my own products and business.

Coaching and consulting is a multi-billion-dollar industry—approximately 20 billion dollars are up for grabs, according to PriceWaterhouseCoopers. And that's just in the USA.

If you hang out with naysayers and losers, they will say the market is saturated. Because there's no dearth of information available online today, you'll feel like everything has been said and done already. That there are already coaches doing what you want to do, that there are already authors who've written books on your subject, that there are thousands of service providers and consultants offering similar services.

The reality is there is also an explosive growth of businesses today. And these businesses need quality help and your help today. Your unique framework, your story, your passion, your unique way of doing things has value. Your vulnerability and your story make you different in a world shifting towards Artificial Intelligence.

It doesn't matter what others are actually doing. You want to put your blinders on, just like racehorses. You want to look forward, not sideways.

It doesn't matter if others are offering similar service, they're not you. Your lived experiences, your way of executing, your way of teaching, your way of education, your way to lead a team and your way of moving people with words could be unique in the world.

Trust that what you *do* matters, and it *will!*

There were plenty of marketing freelancers, and later business coaches, when I started my journey on both counts. People with a really big following, big net worth and they had already made their name in the industry.

It didn't matter to me what others were doing. I knew that my struggles, my failures which I had overcome, my resilience and my intense drive to help people would shine through. When I started posting content online, I had a handful of people listening to me and engaging with my content. There were days when I had nobody show up to my livestreams and webinars. I kept going anyway.

And now, I receive messages on a daily basis from past and current clients about how my programs, courses, mastermind, and services have changed their businesses. My monthly income exploded from $10,000 months to $50,000 months after I added a coaching component.

My mastermind is an annual program where we closely coach and guide entrepreneurs interested in scaling up. We support them with weekly coaching calls, hand holding and community support, quarterly events, accountability to execute and networking opportunities with other amazing mastermind members. We have a cap on the number of clients we service at a time because it's a truly intimate experience and a boutique coaching service. This isn't highly scalable volume-wise as I'm involved in the day-to-day operations of hosting all coaching calls, events and providing community support to our clients.

I've also hosted group coaching programs where we've serviced over 2,000 students at a time. It was more community-based, and the community drives the learning, accountability and inspires everyone to take action. This model is very well-scalable.

I also love to create and sell self-study programs, which

is a brand-new arm of our company. This means there are no coaching calls, but students learn from video training, resources, cheat sheets and rely on executing on their own. This model is highly-scalable and you're able to reach a lot of people with the self-study courses.

Every coaching container is unique and has its pros and cons; you really want to choose something that works well for your lifestyle and priorities. We've executed all containers profitably and guide our mastermind clients on how to choose the best one for them and scale it up based on their priorities.

How Do Coaching Programs Help Clients and Your Business

You are not wrong to think that there is magic in your 1:1 services and clients need 1:1 touchpoint to get their desired results. I used to think that as well. But then I realized the power of group coaching programs—because people get to learn from each via community and peer-to-peer learning. This is in addition to getting to learn from you.

By selling coaching programs that are high-value and high-impact, you get to make a lot of money, reward your team and be responsible for massive customer results. You are turning the same exact framework that's working for your 1:1 clients into a 1: many program so that more clients can go through it at the same time. This gives you an opportunity to leverage your time, and you can build a community of your clients and tell them, *"Hey, let's all work towards these three goals to achieve your desired outcome."*

You coach them on group calls on a weekly basis, and you don't have to do 1:1 calls or 1:1 work anymore. You coach, mentor and guide them on how to do the work, how to implement your framework to get success. They will get better results, because they can go through the program on their time, execute, and come to you for personalized feedback on the group coaching calls.

The community gets better with time. The older community members help the newer clients. The morale and motivation of the community goes to the next level when clients start getting results. They look up to you as a coach, but when they see their peers in the community executing and achieving results with your framework, magic happens!

You've Got This!

If the Universe brought you to this book, and if you have read so far, I know there is a desire burning in your heart to build a company that serves you, your team, your clients, your family and leaves a legacy. It is yours the moment you decide it is.

I've done coaching launches for clients while I was planning my own wedding.
I've run my business when life has brought me to my knees.
I've run it while visiting my in-laws and the responsibilities that come with being a married woman (especially in the Indian culture).
I've run my business while loved ones are suffering.
I've run my business while my face was so swollen with acne that I cried myself to sleep for weeks.
I've run virtual events with a non-ideal office and Wi-Fi setup, while still showing up as my best self to coach.
While Instagram loves to glamorize running a business, real businesses are built by doing the boring work even when it feels like a drag.
I've run my business in all circumstances, ideal and non-ideal.
I've built my business, pivoted, rebuilt stuff so many times.

I'm not a genius, but I can spot some patterns. The last set of billionaires were created from code-based leverage: Bill Gates, Mark Zuckerberg, Elon Musk. The next set of billionaires are being created from Personal Brands: Kim Kardashian, Mr. Beast, Alex Cooper…. and a few amongst you reading this!

Homework: Journal It Out

What inspires you to break out of 1:1 services and build leverage?

What are the topics you're most excited to teach on?

What are the top three outcomes your new coaching program will help your clients with?

Why should they choose you amongst others?

What is your dream price for your program?

Chapter 6

Sell Like It's Your Birthright

I was going through a tough time in my business last year. I felt like I was doing everything in my power to push the business forward but it felt like nothing was happening.

I got a notification from Facebook and I opened to see a mastermind alumnus had messaged me out of the blue. They had been a customer for a couple of years but we hadn't been in touch for months. The message said: *"I just wanted to send you a Thank You note. You are one of those who changed my life. Today I would like to thank you for everything."* The message brought me to tears, because it came when I least expected it and needed it the most.

We think of sales as an icky, sticky, gimmicky thing to do. But the truth is, if I hadn't sold my offers to this client, or to the other 4,000 plus clients, my past and current clients wouldn't be sending me multiple messages like this on a weekly basis.

Selling is helping.
Selling is natural.
Selling is your birthright.

If celebrities are paid millions to talk about other brands in the media, why are you afraid to talk about YOUR brand on YOUR own social media?

I've sold mid-ticket courses, high-end masterminds, and low-ticket self-study programs in my nine-year-long career. I sell each and every product with passion and put my entire heart to it. Even on days when I don't feel like it, I show the fuck up.

The input matters so much more than the output. You can only control the input, nothing else. Your input helps you avoid anxiety, and overthinking. As an unknown wise person on the internet has said: *Overthinking is like a rocking chair. It gives you something to do, but it gets you nowhere.*

Learn sales skills with all your heart. When you learn how to sell you can never go hungry. Whether it is selling yourself in your business or marketing yourself at a job. Sometimes life can be tough, trauma brings you down, or someone betrays you. But they can never take away your skills, your education, your experience, and your ability to sell.

One of the biggest clients I ever worked with became a seven-figure entrepreneur with my help. It was incredible to be a core member of a team that hit multiple million dollars in sales. We were able to utilize my Meta ads and marketing strategies to enroll thousands of clients into the client's online coaching program.

I have also had sales calls with people who are seven/eight/nine-figure entrepreneurs, who have built massive businesses and have first-hand knowledge of how they work in business. And while some of the client deals have fallen through, some other deals have gone through. The losses don't faze me because I like to play the long game in business.

If the deal is not a 'yes' right now, that doesn't mean it is a 'no' forever. Some client deals, especially high-ticket deals could take weeks, months or sometimes even years to close. Buyer psychology is such that someone needs to hear the pitch at least 15 times before purchasing from you, before making a transaction from you.

I have worked with a lot of entrepreneurs across the world, coaching them, consulting them across industries like public relations, life coaching, marketing and freelancing, relationship coaching, mindset coaching, image consulting, sales training and fitness coaching. Every session has been rooted in exchange, each client has taught me something meaningful.

I will tell you that the high-ticket client experience is truly high ticket. They don't nag you, they don't call you 24/7. They don't message you asking for updates. They give you your space, your time, your bandwidth to do the things that they need to do, and most importantly, they trust you. This is very important.

I also believe that anyone can work with high-ticket clients, anyone can charge for their work. It definitely doesn't matter where you are from, what your skin colour is, which religion you practice or if you're an atheist. You just need to be good enough, that's it. But play it cool. In sales, not being desperate is so freakin' important. If you appear desperate, even if you think you're hiding it, it shows in your energy. Be ready to walk away from the deal internally so that you are confident while getting on sales calls. The walk away energy helps you in closing deals.

Get Paid to Build Your Coaching Program

Selling before building is a wise thing to do. You get to craft your offer and test it for a few customers. You get to refine your message and your offer. You're assured it's what the market wants because they paid you for it. Building before selling will lead to months wasted. Building a program is hard work, and that hard work should be done only when the market has validated the offer.

I have sold all my programs via a Founder's Round or a Beta Round. A Founder's Round is when you're selling your idea, not your finished product and collecting early members to say yes to your coaching program. This is smart because instead of wasting months working on your product that no-one might want, we sell our program idea first, get people excited, collect payment and then deliver a smashing program. Getting paid before building something is pretty cool. Customers get better results because you're working with them to seal the cracks in your products. You get testimonials along the way. You get to iterate and make your product better using client feedback.

Group coaching programs are awesome. They are easy to scale, high profit, get the best results, results stack up, alumni help out the newbie clients and a high-value program community is created, which becomes an irreplaceable asset.

Don't get distracted by someone with a million followers selling low-end courses. Don't judge the back-end machine as an outsider. You don't know how the cogs in a wheel work. Likes, Comments, Followers mean nothing if it doesn't translate to a profitable business at the end.

I sold my program Marketing Accelerator at the beta

pricing of $1,000 per unit and sold four spots of it. Whenever you sell to a client, you're promising a program with a start date that is two weeks down the line. That gives you enough time to record module 1 of your program; buckle down, and pre-sell your first 5-10 spots of your program.

While my clients went through Module 1, during week 1, I was one module ahead of them at all times. Then, I took them on an eight-week journey with me while I built the program videos, lectures and cheat sheets based on their questions. I also did weekly coaching calls so I could find gaps in my program, and help them wherever they were stuck with the execution.

I didn't just imagine what they would want from me, I asked them. I created a program that would be a perfect fit for their problems. I taught them my signature framework on how to become a six-figure freelancer based on my personal journey. By the end of the eight-week period, my program was ready. And I had the testimonials and client experiences to share for my marketing campaign. The best part? I got paid $4,000 to build my program without doing any work upfront! I *got paid* to work on my idea!

"What if I create an offer/course but no one buys?"
"What if I put in so much work creating a program and people don't even want it?"

That is why I recommend selling at least 5-10 spots

of your coaching offer before building it…that's the presell formula! To pre-sell your coaching program, do 25-50 sales calls at least and then iterate on the offer and feedback from real customers.

Don't let emotions overrule you. You need a healthy sample size to get a scientific result of an experiment—it can't be done with a few calls and then giving up. Commit to doing at least 25 sales calls for your program.

Why Should You Do Sales Calls at the Start As A Founder

I recommend learning the art of doing sales calls and closing deals on Zoom for your high-end coaching program. You are able to learn the burning pain points that keep your customers up at night. You can't do that by selling via a 'buy now' button on a sales page.

You market your program, ask prospective clients to book sales calls with you, and take them on a journey during the call to help them make the right decision about your program. Being scared and frustrated in the beginning is normal. You will feel like it's not working.

But please remember DATA > EMOTIONS.

Being emotional rather than data driven: There are times in business when I have taken sales rejections personally. If my ads and funnel are not working, I think people hate me and my brand. All that negative self-talk is a drain on my energy and so, I have to remind myself DATA > EMOTIONS! Especially in business.

Focus on your own numbers, data, track everything, be obsessed with data and with your customer results. Put your blinders on, and stop looking at the side. Your only competition is you! You are testing the niche, offer, pricing, sales script, problems—everything. It's hard work. Give yourself grace. Try your best. When you expand the time horizon, it will add up. Don't get emotional and change the offer, pricing, or script, especially when a couple of people tell you the price is too high. Change things up only when you notice a trend with a healthy sample size of at least 25 sales calls.

Distraction is your enemy. Don't get distracted! You will be motivated to do anything but generating and doing sales calls. Sacrifice the short term for the long term—that's how winners operate!

Your Program Offer

Pick one profitable course topic, you don't need multiple courses. I would argue that one right high-ticket offer is needed to hit your first million dollars.

If you have multiple ideas, pick the idea you're most excited about. You can and will absolutely launch more coaching programs in your career as a coach. Focus is necessary to get started and go *all in* on one offer.
Choose the idea that is at the intersection of these three

things: what you're most excited to teach, which offer will solve people's most annoying problems, which offer will people will pay me the best for. For example: voice coaching program for actors/speakers, communication skills program for corporate employees/founders/ executive, client attraction program for freelancers/ agency owners.

Your Program Price

In the same niche, people sell $50 courses as well as $3,000 courses as well.

What's different? The clientele! Offer outcomes! The mindset! The results! If you sell a $10,000 fitness program to an ordinary gym-going person, they might not see the value in it. If the program is sold to an aspiring Olympic athlete, now that's a no-brainer. Who you sell it to is the most important decision you'll make.

How to Sell on Sales Calls

Here is the eight-step sales process to close 30-40 percent of the calls you're going on. My mastermind goes in-depth into sharing sales mindset, scripts and more, but here is a glimpse of the entire process.

Step 1: Re-affirm why they booked a call
Step 2: Learn about their current situation in detail
Step 3: Learn about their desired situation in detail
Step 4: Create a bridge between their current and desired

situation, with examples
Step 5: Learn what they have done to fix this gap and solve this problem
Step 6: Learn why they are unable to fix this on their own
Step 7: Share your offer with a customized pitch that narrows the gap between their current and desired situation
Step 8: Affirm why they need to take action now

Why Didn't They Buy?

Now, let's talk about why someone won't buy from you:

Time Objection:
"I'm busy right now."
"In this season too much is happening."

Here you want to share a plan on how investing 30 minutes or 60 minutes per day can bring them closer to their goals. Share a plan of how to go about time management along with your offer of how they can meet their goals faster. Share how they might waste even more time trying to figure out the solution on their own, or it might take longer without the accountability you are offering inside your program.

"I don't have time to implement."

Give them a time management plan, or offer to actually do the work for them and charge them for the 'done for you' service.

Price Objection:
"I don't have the budget."

In most cases, they don't value the offer to justify the pricing. That means you need to do a better job of connecting how they can solve their pain points, and achieve their desired transformation in a simplified manner with your help.

If it's truly a budget issue, introduce pay plans or EMI options. Don't use discounts, use the pain points that they shared to twist the knife on the urgency of why they need to take action today to get closer to their desired situation.

"You don't understand me."

They won't say this on the call, but they're thinking it to themselves and making excuses. They think you didn't understand their problems. Talk about the outcomes, and their pain points and ask if you can answer any lingering questions. Make sure you're making a personalized pitch based on their dreams, and pain points.

"I don't trust the brand/offer."

They won't say this on the call, but they're thinking it to themselves and making excuses. This implies a lack of social proof or trust or value that wasn't shared. Send them a playlist of the client case studies, try to get the main truth out and then deal with the objection.

"I'm looking at options."

Your competitor might just be a better fit for them so let your marketing get them back in your world via your ads, social media content and email marketing.

"I need to think about it, I need to talk to the spouse/parent."

Book a second sales call once they've talked to another decision maker. Or offer to bring the decision maker on the next call. Ask them, "Does the same time work two days from now?" If someone shows up on the second call, closes are highly likely.

It could be one objection as to why they didn't purchase, or a combination of objections. You want to audit each one of your sales calls from the above list, and figure out what could be the root cause. Follow-up after a sales call is super important as well. I love reaching out via audio messages on Instagram to know how close they are to enrollment.

Remember: Always, get the TRUTH out on sales calls.

Once per quarter, follow up with your old leads/old calls and get them on a second call to re-sell them. I like to do a follow-up three times and then stop—let your marketing inspire them to come back to you.

My mastermind, Vortex, is well known to cover my best performing sales scripts, objection handling, and closing psychology. If you need my personalized help and training to upskill yourself, consider applying to join us.

How I Sell Everyday

There was a time when I used to beat myself up over how much money my company was making every month at the time. Whatever my company made never felt "enough". I used to obsessively calculate numbers, create Excel sheets and projections on what launches are supposed to look like and how each subsequent month had to double the current month, if not perform better. I used to assign meaning to what certain offer launches did or did not do. And I used to assign my self-worth to those numbers. *Not anymore.*

I know that a launch not going well, doesn't mean it's going to be a bad quarter or a bad year. I don't overanalyze or beat myself up for it. I look for data and make decisions based on data rather than emotions.

Data > Emotions

I launch my offers and products with all my heart. I take smart, inspired actions to support the launch. I create content and create funnels congruent with the message I wish to deliver to my audience. That solves my audience's problem at the time. I trust that whoever is called to the offers will join in at the perfect time. Whether that time is now or later, it's none of my concern. That's why I don't like to be pushy in my marketing or on sales calls. I believe in attraction rather than chasing.

I've been known to say to my loved ones: *"You can get everything you want in life. Just not on your timeline."*

You don't know how many clients jump on sales calls with me or my team, and say they have silently been following my content over the years. And they have been so inspired by me. Then, they continue to pay in full for my high-ticket mastermind. Most of the time, they haven't even purchased anything low-ticket from me ever. It always shocks me how little we think of our own work or impact.

We feel like no one is listening or watching our content. And no one will ever buy from us. I didn't even know these people existed and today they're my best clients. If this doesn't inspire you to keep going with your content creation journey on social media, I don't know what will.

How To Build a Brand

Instead of caring about the number of followers, likes, audience you have now and will have in the future, focus on serving. Serving that one customer you have, providing value to the 100 followers you have right now, and making sure you're showing up to serve rather than focusing on fame, money or any other motivator.

That's the mistake everyone makes going into this, I get so many Instagram messages in the lines of:

"Roota, how do I become rich?"

"How can I get 100K followers?"

"How do I build a personal brand?"

And the very first question I ask them is this: *"How are you helping people? What value can you provide to them?"*

If you cannot take care of your 100 followers right now, and serve them, you do not deserve 1 million followers. Success starts small. Don't go out there looking to become rich and famous instantly. Be ready to put in a lot of work, serve your audience, help them better their lives, and see not just your follower count go up but also watch your revenue grow.

Mr. Beast started his channel in 2012, when he was a teenager at school. It took him five years of producing bad videos to finally create one that performed decently. I applied the same principle, and went from having 400-something followers to more than 350K followers across social media platforms, as of today. I have a community who not just likes my posts, but also buys my products, implements them, and gets results.

Like many of you, I had a personal Instagram account with 200-something followers a decade ago. I had decided I was going to be a travel blogger and write about my travels within India and abroad. I loved taking pretty pictures and being creative with my captions. The Purple Backpack Instagram account went from 0 to 5,000 followers in a few short months. That was my first stint with posting on social media and getting some momentum from it. I made use of engagement pods, hashtags, did follow for follows, being in a community of other travel bloggers who supported each other's content—and literally asking anyone who will listen to follow me. I did everything short of buying followers—I have never done that and I won't recommend it to anyone.

When I want to achieve a goal, I do *everything.* Everything possible that will work. I prefer to go *all in,* and get as much data as possible.

Build a Community Instead

Attach yourself to people.
Build offers that help them.
The Brand, the money, the success will flow.

Focus on building community, don't chase follower

numbers. Engaged followers matter much more than your follower account. Engaged followers mean people who actually engage with your content and support it daily. Engaged followers can also be compared to what the former editor of *Wired* magazine, Kevin Kelly, calls the '1,000 true fans' concept. These followers support you no matter what niche you're currently creating content in, no matter what pivots you make, and they consistently purchase your products.

Learning to build a community has been a skill that has paid off. I remember when I was running my first program, and was serving 2,200 students actively, people appreciated the community the most. That Facebook group was positive, uplifting, extremely helpful, and was the catalyst to getting so many client results.

To host a successful community, you, the host, have to put in a lot upfront. You have to portray yourself in a way that assures people that you're not the cult leader of the group; instead, you're just a facilitator connecting everyone inside. Even if you stop posting in the community for months, the conversation and the community energy still must keep going.

Community building is a many: many relationship rather than a 1: many relationship that you would have with your Instagram follower or a YouTube subscriber. Everyone helps each other, there's peer relationships, and they love hanging out together—whether you're present or not. Currently, our mastermind community is the place to be. Our mastermind clients meet up for coffee and dinner in their cities, take trips together without me knowing or being a part of those meetups. Some of these clients have become lifelong friends.

I created a safe space where everyone feels comfortable being vulnerable with their business problems, and everyone uplifts each other. There's no negativity or jealousy in this community. We collectively believe: if one person wins, everyone wins. Today, if you feel like you're missing having a community in your life or business, it's a sign to start one of your own. You can choose whichever platform you like best; I love Skool.

For the first three months of starting your community, over-deliver. Do weekly coaching or accountability calls, organize meetups in cities, or Zoom co-working sessions to collaborate, run challenges in your communities, and get five people to start being engaged community members. Community building is a long-term goal. Don't expect to monetize it immediately. You have to put in sweat equity first to reap long-term benefits.

Once you have built an audience, you need to know the art of selling. Selling is how businesses thrive and survive. There's nothing wrong with selling your products and services as long as they help people and are created with honesty and integrity.

Think Long-term in Business

It's incredible to think that my first program went on to serve more than 2,200 students all over the world. My students called it better than an MBA degree, and have leveraged the frameworks inside to get high-end clients, scale up their digital businesses, land marketing jobs across the world and gain control of their day.

Students started hitting $1,000 months and $5,000 months in their freelance business, so it's not like I was just making money off my course. But our students were also learning new skills, becoming independent and working with premium international clients. This is what brought me the most joy.

We start small. By starting my own Facebook group, going on Instagram lives, my failed travel blog, the client gigs which felt tough… all of these were adding up slowly and steadily. This decision, of diving into the unknown, quitting my job was life-changing for me. Then leaving my 1:1 freelance business, and building leverage with my 1: many programs changed my life for the second time.

Without it, I won't be running a million-dollar company today.

This is my story from the start to today. But there were a lot of lessons and failures learnt along the way. Today, I operate by creating long-term goals and vision for my company. I have a document with my long-term vision and goals in my Google drive, and every time I read it, it gives me goosebumps. The weird part is that I am not even close to achieving any of those goals right now. But I feel fabulous and even more inspired when I read them. It's not enough to simply dream with my eyes open, I have to nurture the dream as well.

This also leads you to stop assigning goal deadlines, which I believe is the villain in every entrepreneur's life. Stop thinking, *"Oh, if I don't achieve a $100,000 launch in the next five days, it means I'm a failure."* Nope, it doesn't.

When you create long-term goals, you feel inspired to work towards them slowly and learn to give yourself time. You're no longer in a rush to hit small milestones and swiftly post on social media to celebrate. You toil and work hard behind the scenes for years to then share your work with the world. Just like my favourite inspirations, authors like Robin Sharma, or musical artists like Taylor Swift, or cinematic geniuses like Christopher Nolan, do. They disappear into their art for years, until they have something truly worthwhile to share with the world.

This means that if and when that product launch doesn't really hit your exact number goal for any reason, you're able to calm down and tell yourself that you're building something big. And everything you do is bringing you closer to it, one day at a time.

Everything you do today is a wealthy move.
Every post you publish.
Every message conversation with a prospective client.
Every coaching call that you do.
Every problem you solve for your clients.
Every roadblock you unblock for your clients.
Every sales call that you do.
Every email you sent out.
Every video that you put out.
Every ad campaign you launch.
Every team member you hire and train and nurture.
It's all counting towards that big beautiful brand that stands the test of time.

Homework

Start making noise about your first or next coaching program: write a social media post, email or start a Meta ads campaign. You don't need to build it right now, you need to pre-sell it first.

Ask people to come on calls with you. Talk to at least 25 people. Message me on Instagram when you close your first few clients so I can celebrate with you!

Start a community about a topic that you're passionate about. Collect like-minded people inside that community. You'll learn skills on the go.

Chapter 7

Your Million-Dollar Business

Sometimes you have to burn the ship, leap into the ocean, and start swimming forward…even if you don't know where you're going.

Here's the truth:
No one came to me and asked me to start a travel blog on the side with my job.
No one asked me to quit my job even when I had zero clue about what's next.
No one told me it was time to start getting my first few freelance clients.
No one told me to start selling my first coaching program.
No one asked me to write this book.
No one knocked my door down, shook me, said "Roota

you gotta do this, people are begging and waiting for this."

I did it, because *I decided it was time.*

I believe the people who have a backup plan, tend to not give their 1,000 per cent to make it work.
I knew I didn't want to work in a corporate job ever again.
I knew I didn't want to commute to work and be stuck for hours in traffic daily.
I knew I didn't want to force myself to go to the office when I was sick.
I knew I didn't want to work on projects that left me creatively wanting more.
I knew I didn't want to work where I didn't know if my work was making any impact at all.
I knew I didn't want to work 14-hour-days and be lost in an employee count of thousands.
I knew I didn't want to work to make somebody else richer.

So, I built a company which would be life-first for me. I didn't purchase a fancy car or a home in my 20s. I invested all my profits back into my business—to learn, to grow, to pay for automation tools, to pay for client experience, to pay salaries and bonuses to my team, to invest in my own learning via masterminds.

I remember wanting to give up countless times throughout the journey especially when I had to deal with the income ups and downs, tough clients, haters, naysayers, and a ton of self-doubt. I have no marketing or business degree. I'm self-taught in business. No-one taught me how to build a million-dollar company. I learnt by soaking in from my mentors like a sponge, and executing every single day for years.

Recently in my business, the yearly taxes I've paid are more than the yearly salary I had back in my well-paid software engineer job. It's been a journey. The week I hit my first million dollars in my company, I bought a beautiful peach bag at the Chanel boutique in Dubai. I gifted it to myself and I was so proud of my journey that day.

I love the company I have built. I love that it has brought me safety and security and fulfillment. And it has helped me make life-changing money. It has led to multiple clients of mine running a six-figure-business or seven-figure business (in USD) today, and have huge brands online that you may know or have heard of. It has led to my clients being able to buy homes, cars, taking their parents on luxury vacations, and have enough financial security for themselves. It has led to me paying salaries and giving bonuses and sharing profits with multiple team members, largely women, over the years.

I have a social media manager, a video editor, a graphic designer, an accountant and more people including funnel designers, editors, publicists I hire when the need arises. As I hire others, my time and energy is freed up to do the things only I can do in my company—writing, creating videos, and coaching clients.

It has led me to donate to multiple charitable organizations which help children with food and education; those that rehabilitate sex workers and trafficked women; others, which help save coral reefs all over the world. My dream and hope for you is that you build your company exactly the way you want to. That you sell whatever it is that you want (with integrity, of course), and you get to sell at whatever pricing that lights you up.

But you can't help the poor if you are poor. Know that making more than enough money for yourself is the only way to make the world a better place. You have to first help yourself before you help others.

How to Start Your Coaching Business

One of our clients was stuck charging $30 per hour for 1:1 singing coaching sessions. She was burnt out because she was doing 1:1 coaching for nearly 10 hours a day and still wasn't able to make her dream monthly revenue.

She implemented what I'm about to tell you in this chapter, and launched a group coaching program to leverage her time better. She now runs a relaxed business, works with serious clients only, and sells a $1,000 group program helping professional singers

prepare for the performance industry.
Building a coaching business is incredibly rewarding. If you'd like to build one, here are a few questions I would like you to answer:

Which problems have you overcome in your own life or business?
What are one or two problems that you are most excited to help others with?
Why do you want to create a course or a coaching program?
What outcomes do you help people achieve?
What problems does your program solve?
Who do you want to solve it for and what is the price point you are thinking of during this transformation from point A to point B?
Why do people want to buy from you?
Have you accomplished the transformation yourself or have others achieved results with it?

If you're thinking: *"Roota, I don't have enough followers. Is it the right time to start building and selling my program?"* I'm here to tell you that no, you don't need to wait. Five of my mastermind clients who have crossed six figures in their business have less than 2,000 followers. It truly doesn't matter, *unless you let it.* I want this book to be evergreen, and so I won't name platforms at this point. This works regardless of which platform you choose to show up on.

If I had 0 followers today, here's what I'd do to grow

my following and profits:

- Make your social media profiles optimized to share clear outcomes that help your target audience.

- Post 60-second videos daily, and post on all social media platforms available to you. Create shareable and savable content!

- Send 20-30 friend/follow requests everyday so new people are introduced to your content.

- Engage with people's content for 30 minutes every day to nurture relationships.

- Social selling on DMS every day! Invite people to DM you, learn their problems, share your transformation framework with them, invite them to book a call with you.

- Work hard to get one video case study from your clients.

- Build an email list so you can convert everyone to an owned audience. Do not build a business on rented land.

- Social media platforms can take your followers away, but no one can touch your email list. Send emails every day to generate sales calls!

- Go on sales calls and close because followers don't matter the most, sales do.

Build a Community Instead of Chasing Followers

I've grown a couple of communities in the past and I still am building a couple of communities right now.

One of the best stories that I can think of is the Marketing Accelerator community, which was a signature course that I sold a couple of years ago. It amassed 2,200 clients across 14 countries and the client impact across it has been nothing short of a miracle. Client sales account for $16 million dollars in impact.

If I have to give you an idea about what made the program successful, it was not just the training, which, I admit I'm a bit biased towards, but something more. And it was not just the weekly calls from me, my team and the coaches. I would attribute the success of a program to the community, the level of community that you create, for your audience, and for your clients. Community-based learning is a gamechanger, it is the future. It is the best way to learn because it fosters the right level of competition, where people get inspired from each other rather than thinking and stealing from each other's plate. There is no negativity if it is built right.

Everyone benefits from everyone's knowledge. For instance, look at the Paypal Mafia. Paypal Mafia was a group of founders who were working together on scaling Paypal, who later went on to start their own successful companies, like Elon Musk, Peter Theil and more.

A lot of successful people sustain their success because of who they surround themselves with. *Proximity is power.* So, the best thing you can do for your courses, coaching programs and masterminds is focused on building the community vibe. Your clients are able to make friends, they are able to get accountability partners, they feel less lonely in this journey of entrepreneurship. Our Vortex Mastermind is an excellent example of this.

Entrepreneurship is Not a Cakewalk

In one of his social media posts, Alex Hormozi, the Iranian-American serial entrepreneur, investor, and philanthropist, wrote: *"Expect that it's going to take longer than you think, cost more than you think and will take more work than you think."*

I'm not here to paint entrepreneurship as a bed of roses. Business is tough. You have to hire and fire people. You have to deal with long-term team members leaving. You have to constantly keep your guard up. You have to constantly be on the hunt for deals. You have to sometimes sacrifice other areas of life to gain an edge. You have to learn to not be complacent. You have to be humble. You have to have enough ego to keep fighting the war. You have to be kind. You have to deal with haters, trolls, negativity and naysayers. You have to deal with unsupportive loved ones. You have to keep going even after falling down a million times. You have to be your own coach and hype guru again and again.

But at the end of the day, I won't have it any other way and I can't imagine myself doing anything else.

Your Days as a CEO

My freelancer days looked like this: preparing for a sales call with a client, conducting the sales call, sending invoices and contracts, writing a sales page for a product I was launching for the client, creating and launching ad campaigns, publishing content for different clients, and engaging in outreach and relationship building within Facebook groups for lead generation.

Now, my days have a different focus: closing higher-ticket clients into a mastermind, recording new lectures and training sessions for our clients, reviewing applications for our mastermind, conducting weekly Vortex mastermind coaching calls, checking on client results and progress, hand hold clients who require additional help and working on various new projects within our company such as a new funnel, writing a book or launching a new self-study program for our audience. I also spend a couple hours per week recording video content that my team then distributes all across social media platforms.

That's the fun part of doing business. You can choose to delegate the tasks which are not your forte or tasks which you don't enjoy doing. You get to choose how your day looks like as a CEO.

Do You Need a Website?

When I was moving from making $5,000 a month to aiming for $10,000, did I have a website? Yes, absolutely. Was it super fancy or professional? Not really, but it was there. I'd definitely recommend having a website if you're in that range or aiming to get there.

While a website won't instantly supercharge your income, it's great for branding and building trust. You can monitor your visitors, add Meta tracking pixels and retarget visitors using ads and use Google Analytics to gain insights from your website traffic. A website helps indirectly by giving you a central spot for your testimonials, social proof, and offers. It gives you a chance to start an email newsletter, and email list building is important for consistently hitting $10,000 months.

Making $10,000 a month once can be relatively easy—it could be a fluke or just good timing. But maintaining that level consistently requires a solid strategy.

You can leverage your email list to generate sales for your small offers and sales calls for your bigger offers on demand. Growing your email list should be a top priority. Even right now, as I'm writing this, it's still the best way to generate calls and sell high-ticket offers. Most of our sales calls for our high-end programs—about 90 per cent—come from our email list, which we use to convert leads into clients. So, having your email list is key. Make it your top priority, and then focus on your website.

When I hit my first $10,000 a month, my website was a simple sales page where I shared what clients could expect from my services, showcased social proof, and included past case studies. I also had a basic Calendly link for scheduling calls. On these calls, I would ask questions about their monthly profit and revenue, their goals, and their current and desired lead generation and calls.

Scaling Up from $10,000 Months

I want to be real with you, I can share the principles and framework for you right now, but the social media, marketing and advertising landscape changes monthly, so I reserve the updated practical strategy for my programs and mastermind. Otherwise, it's a disservice to you to read outdated information in the book, and my goal is to write an evergreen book for you.

So, after hitting the $10,000 month target a few times—three or four months in a row—I wanted to grow further, so I explored coaching. I decided to teach others how to become freelancers, develop essential skills, and attract international clients from all over the world for these skills. Just like I did.

Having clients from your existing network can be really valuable. All of my freelancing clients were international, mainly from the US, UK, Australia, or Canada. Having 95 per cent of my clients from international markets was a unique part of my journey. International clients tend to pay well, treat you professionally, and stick to deadlines. It was a joy to work with them because everything was handled smoothly and respectfully. That said, local markets can be just as good. In our mastermind group, for example, we have a predominantly Indian clientele, and my experience of coaching them has been excellent.

It really comes down to the mindset you bring to your work. Good clients exist everywhere. While you should set boundaries to ensure clients don't take advantage of you, high-ticket prices remain high-ticket prices, no matter where you are. Whether a client is paying $5,000 from India, the US, or Australia, it's still $5,000. Money is universal. So, I wouldn't favour one market over another or change my offer for different regions. I keep a single offer and try to sell it to anyone who is a good fit. The key is ensuring they are the right niche and that you can genuinely help them.

At this point, I was transitioning from 1:1 agency freelance work to coaching because I wanted to make more money while working less. Handling five 'done for you' marketing clients by myself was a lot of work. It was good money, almost all of it was profit since I had no major expenses, but it was still tough. 1:1 agency work can be demanding, and I didn't see myself running a million-dollar marketing agency handling 20 team members all at once. I could see myself enjoying running my coaching business, sharing my video training, doing live events, writing books, and helping my clients achieve their desired transformation. That truly lit up my heart.

Remember, from my college days when I landed that internship teaching eighth grade kids, I knew educating others was what I was made for. Yes, I could have hired a team and scaled up to a full-blown agency model—plenty of people do that. It just wasn't one of my goals. Ever since I was young, I wanted to make a more personal impact and help people directly with my experience.

Here, you have to think with discernment instead of following the herd, and ask yourself, *what is it that I should do?* Am I doing it because others are doing it or am I doing it because it's what I truly want? I've seen a lot of entrepreneurs burn out because they don't use their discernment as a CEO and make their own decisions. Learn from your mentors, get inspired from your heroes, but do what is right for you and your lifestyle.

Coaching came naturally to me, and I haven't looked

back since. I've been a coach for about eight years now, and my coaching style is unique because I focus on mindset first. I'm all about making lasting changes rather than chasing after quick fixes or trendy strategies that only work for a short time. I believe in building long-lasting skills and a strong foundation. For example, if you learn sales, you can apply those principles anywhere, no matter the market or technology. Sales and marketing fundamentals remain constant. I don't believe in constantly chasing crazy revenue numbers month after month because I've done that in the past and realised that it doesn't bring happiness, only stress.

It's important to decide which number truly makes you happy. For some people, it's $10,000 a month; for others, it's $50,000, $100,000, or even $1 million a month. There's no right or wrong amount—it's about what works for you. Remember, some people will always earn more, and some will earn less. This isn't a race you can win; sometimes, you have to pause and decide when to stop running and enjoy the journey. It's easy to fall into a new kind of hamster wheel. Just like when you're climbing the corporate ladder for promotions and titles, as an entrepreneur, you might find yourself constantly chasing new revenue goals. The pressure to grow 200 per cent year over year can make you feel like a failure if you don't meet those expectations. All the hustle culture and competitive marketing can be overwhelming. Personally, I've stepped away from that game.

When I was in the $10,000 range, I was definitely driven and eager to achieve more quickly. I was hungry for growth and wanted to expand beyond just 1:1 clients. I didn't find $10,000 enough; I wanted to scale up. So, I started a transition from 1:1 services to offering 1:many solutions.

First 100 Coaching Students

For anyone out there in that transition phase of going from 1:1 to 1:many, don't worry—you can absolutely do it! If you already have the following, that's fantastic. It gives you a great head start and allows you to sell more and manage more. But even if you don't have a big following, selling a few spots at a high-ticket price is still very achievable.

During the transition from making $10,000 to $25,000 a month, I had one major 1:1 marketing client who was paying me around $4,000 a month. That income covered all my bills, paid for my team members, and covered the costs for software and ads to scale the course. I was happy with that arrangement and didn't take on any additional clients.

Over the course of a year, my income grew significantly, making it clear that it was time to move away from 1:1 work. I had to let go of that client, even though they didn't want me to leave. We'd worked together for almost two years, but I needed to focus on growing my brand and scaling my course.

Don't let anyone—whether it's social media, family members, competitors, or anyone else—tell you otherwise. Opportunities are still very much available; the market is not saturated.

After launching my course, I worked with my initial group of students over an eight-week period. We held weekly online classes via Zoom, and I was there to answer all their questions. By the end of the course, I had some great case studies and decided to expand my reach.

Then, I took the course I recorded and launched it in the Indian market at a lower price point of $300. The response was fantastic! In the very first launch, we had 25 students, which brought in $7,500. This was a big jump from the $4,000 I made in the initial beta launch.

I increased the price in the subsequent launches. By the second launch in the Indian market, we had 40-50 new students. The price went up to $400, and the course remained at that price, all through 2019. By then, I had approximately 100 students. I remember looking back at some notes on my vision board where I had written "100 *MAA* students by the end of this year"—it was amazing to see that dream come true.

As the course gained momentum, I realized I needed help. So, I hired someone to assist with client execution and administration tasks related to the course. This person was actually one of my students. I posted a hiring announcement in my community, interviewed candidates, and eventually brought someone on board. When you're in a transition phase and need support, hiring someone can be a great move. You can train them, and it doesn't have to be expensive. I started with a part-time intern and paid them around $300 to $500 a month, which was quite reasonable at the time.

I always prefer hiring interns, training them, and then evaluating their performance after a few months to see if they're a good fit for a long-term role. If yes, I would see how things went from there. I gradually created a three-person part-time team.

However, I wouldn't necessarily recommend that approach to you today. If you find one part-time person who is exceptional, it's often better to promote them to a full-time position. Having one reliable full-timer can be much more efficient than managing several part-timers. It simplifies training, leaves, and other administrative tasks, which can pile up with multiple people.

Even though managing part-time team members was a bit challenging, it was a great experience. Some of my best team members came during that period. With the course gaining traction, I started hitting consistent monthly earnings of $20,000 to $25,000, which felt encouraging to me.

The secret to hitting $25,000 months consistently was automations.

Funnels, Automations and Ads

Turning on funnel and automations to turn my coaching program to make evergreen sales was a turning point.

A funnel is a journey you take a stranger on to build trust, have them share their email information with you, to book a call with you, to purchase from you.

Depending on your price point, the call stage can be removed and you can make a direct purchase pitch. A funnel can include videos, ads, emails, series of webpages, multiple offers along the way, live training and more. There are a lot of permutations possible in which funnels work for a particular niche and price point.

It's crazy to think that with our own proprietary automation and funnel frameworks, our mastermind program has helped so many of our clients build $100,000-$300,000 businesses using these exact frameworks. By integrating Facebook ads with my automated video funnel, I was able to generate revenue around the clock. It was incredible!

At one point, we were making a sale every single day, and on our best days, we'd get three sales daily—about 30 sales a month. This translated to 90-100 new customers each month. That's the real power of an evergreen funnel.

With time, I raised the price of the program to $600, and then later $700, so you can do the math of how much we were doing in those months. When I had everything running smoothly—my ads performing well, the funnel dialled in, and everything tested—it felt amazing. That's what I consider true freedom: making money on autopilot. It's as close to passive income as you can get, even though I don't fully believe in a complete passive income.

For the next couple of years, we averaged around $50,000 a month. But we had one standout month where we hit $88,000, thanks to a successful live launch. It was heartening to see how the sales grew from one a day to two, then three per day. It was like discovering a whole new level of automation and efficiency. Funnels lead to evergreen sales without needing to do more than just maintenance.

Evergreen Funnels

I want to share a bit about how I managed my evergreen funnel. During that time, the funnel was running around the clock—24/7, without breaks for festivals or weekends. It was making sales constantly. But, at the end of each quarter, we would run a big organic launch.

Here's how it worked: in the first two months of the quarter, people would come in and buy through ads. They would click on an ad, watch our free training, and then a percentage of viewers would convert to customers. Some would make a purchase right away, while others needed more time to think about it. By the third month, we'd conduct a major launch. Typically, this involved a big webinar or a series of emails with enticing bonuses, which drew a lot of sales from people who didn't take action immediately.

This approach helped us improve our overall return on ad spend for the quarter and made the campaign very profitable. So, if you're using an evergreen funnel, I highly recommend supplementing it with a live launch, once a quarter. Even now, I like to run three-day virtual event funnels, which I cover in detail in Vortex Mastermind. You can find all the information on how to execute this inside the mastermind.

Live launches, two-four times a year, can really sequence the juice of the evergreen funnels and convert fence sitters to become customers. I love teaching the evergreen and live launch "hybrid" model to our mastermind clients because every business is unique and you truly want to deploy the funnel/automation that works best for your specific offer.

Million-dollar Systems and Teams

Let's talk about building a million-dollar team—because empires aren't built alone. Here are three simple rules that I have used to hire dozens of employees over the last nine years:

- Hire when it pains, not before.

- Hire slowly, fire quickly.
- Consider hiring for a paid internship for three months. Observe their performance, provide support, then evaluate their potential for full-time roles.

Conduct quarterly reviews and regular 1:1 meetings with your team members, preferably monthly, so you're in touch with them. Once, I had five team members simultaneously, and while I thought they were all necessary, managing them became challenging. From this, I learned that hiring skilled people and rewarding them well leads to higher efficiency. Instead of five or six people, you might need just two exceptional individuals for businesses aiming for consistent monthly revenues of $50,000 to $100,000. Keep your team lean, focused, and efficient for a simple, profitable, and relaxed business.

This advice is perfect for coaching and consulting businesses but might not apply to building a software or tech company. With respect to employee skills, I prefer the software engineering 'Full Stack' approach, where team members are trained in multiple areas. While they specialize in one or two areas, they possess a generalist mindset and can contribute well across various areas.

I've realized that firing employees is something I really dislike doing. But it's important to be a leader and get it done. Procrastinating firing someone can negatively impact the team culture and morale. The longer you delay, the greater the disruption. Rip off the Band-Aid: show clarity to your existing team and answer their questions without hiding anything. For the employee leaving: show kindness and give them all the support they need. Provide a severance package, testimonials, and recommendations to assist them in finding new opportunities.

I was able to build a million-dollar company by focusing on systems and processes: It's essential to have Standard Operating Procedures (SOPs) in place. Develop SOPs for various aspects, including customer service, sales, launch processes, and ad campaigns. These documents serve as valuable references for your team. Create both written and video instructions in Google Sheets or Docs. You don't need a fancy project management tool unless you have a big team.

I like to keep it simple with my tech stack. The tools that fuel my business include Zoom, Slack, Google Suite, Zapier, and Calendly. These are the bare minimum which you might need as well. On top of this, you might need a funnel builder like Leadpages, and an email customer relationship management tool like Kit.

Challenges are Redirection

In 2020, the COVID-19 pandemic hit, and my evergreen course sales came to a halt. It was a scary time, but we quickly adapted. We updated our ad messaging to address the situation and highlighted how people could benefit from upskilling and taking our courses.

This adjustment helped us not only recover but also usher in some of our best performances in 2020 and 2021. Online education boomed during that period, and although there was a slight decline afterward, I still am bullish about the power and impact of online education.

Can You Still Make a Million Dollars Today?

You might have some questions like, *"Is it still possible to stand out as a service provider, freelancer or coach right now?"* The answer is yes! People have been asking this question every year—2018, 2019, 2020, and so on. The concern is always the same, but here's the truth: transactions are happening every day. The economy is always moving. People spend money on coffee, groceries, gym memberships, and more.

Money circulates constantly.

With over 8 billion people on the planet and more people gaining Internet access every day, there continues to be a vast amount of potential. The only thing that can limit you is your mindset. There's a lot of money and transactions happening out there, and everyone deserves a slice of it.

Think about it: Apple is a trillion-dollar company and continues to grow. If a giant like Apple can keep expanding, there's no reason we can't hit $10,000,

$20,000, or even $50,000 a month. We have the entire world at our fingertips. There are plenty of clients, businesses needing help, and opportunities to make an impact. If you don't help them, someone else will.

In 2025 and beyond, content is key. Your unique brand, voice, and story can help you stand out. By sharing your journey, struggles, and solutions, you can build a community and become the go-to expert in your niche. There were times when I had family emergencies and couldn't work for two full months. Despite that, sales kept rolling in, and my team managed everything seamlessly. I wasn't able to create content or launch anything during that period, but the funnel and the team took care of everything.

Having a 1:many offer is incredibly valuable because it means your business doesn't solely depend on you being present. If your business only makes money when you're actively involved, then it's just another job you've created for yourself. In my opinion, a good business should keep running smoothly even when you're not directly involved.

There's plenty of money to be made beyond just the usual price ranges. Can you charge $2,000 a month? Absolutely. What about $5,000 a month? Yes. $10,000 a month? Definitely. Even $100,000 a month? Again, yes. The key is whether the value you offer justifies the price. That's what really matters—pricing becomes secondary once you've established the value you provide.

I genuinely hope this is enough inspiration for you to begin the transition from your 1:1 journey to launching your own high-end coaching program because it truly changed the game for me and my clients. I'd say launching my coaching program was a wealthy move I'm forever grateful I made.

Homework: Create a Game Plan and Start Executing

One offer, one funnel, one traffic source is the key to hitting your first million. Map out that offer that gives you this leverage.

Which platforms are you most excited to post on and start running ads on?

Are there any lies you're telling yourself about making a million-dollars in today's economy? Journal them out.

Start your community today, instead of worrying about growing your followers. It can be a free Facebook group, a Skool community, or a WhatsApp community. Show up, be vulnerable and help people to connect with each other within your community.

Chapter 8

Million-Dollar Money Mindset

I come from a small town, from a middle-class family, and we didn't have a lot when I was growing up. Vacations were far and few, once every few years or so; and whenever we did go, it was always about getting a deal and negotiating a better price for every single thing. Or taking the hardest and longest possible way to reach somewhere to save money. Vacations felt like a lot of work back then. So, when I started to have a disposable income, I wanted to spend money to relax on vacations—choosing to take a flight over a train or bus, to spend the day lying around by the pool in the resort if I felt like it, instead of trying to "make the best" of the vacation by scheduling 10 things to do or see during the day; and to choose more expensive experiences without worrying about money.

I want to talk about money mindset because I know you would also have learned some stuff about money in your formative years, which might be limiting your tendencies to make more money, or sustain the money that you earn, and even enjoy the money that you make. Unlearning the stuff which you learnt during childhood, which hinders your money mindset is crucial.

You might have heard that rich people are evil, that there are no ethical billionaires. I echo what Amanda Frances writes in her book *Rich As F*ck: More Money Than You Know What to Do With:* "Money is neither good nor bad. It is a neutral asset."

Yes, money in the hands of the wrong people is absolutely bad. Bad people do bad things with money. But good people do good things with money. When you make more money with your business, it allows you to help people. It allows your team to pay for their bills, buy food, buy a home or whatever their family needs. It allows you and your family safety, security and happiness. It allows you to donate to charitable causes that are close to your heart. It allows you to actually make a difference in the world. Having money doesn't make you a bad person. If you do good things with money, you will keep making more money. If you do evil things with money, karma will get you.

If your mindset doesn't believe the above things or there's some resistance, figure out the reason why.
Did something that happened in your childhood cause

this resistance?
Does some false story about money affect you even now?
What would it take to unlearn that story and trust a new reality about money?
What if having money would increase your safety, security and happiness?

I highly recommend journaling to answer some of the questions at this point. If you don't release these money blocks, it would be difficult to make your peace with making money, as well as maintaining that money.

My husband built his wealth by being an early employee in a tech startup that went on to be a large publicly-traded company. He came from humble beginnings and when I met him, he had an ordinary job. He made wealthy moves along the way and paved his way to success from scratch. In the 14 years I have known him, I've never heard him say:

I can't afford that.
I can't buy that.
I don't have money for that.
This is too expensive for me.

He unintentionally trained his mind to think wealthy thoughts. He doesn't read books or read money psychology books. I, on the other hand, have intentionally trained my brain to focus on positive money thoughts such as:

This purchase is chill, it's so easy.
I can pay off my home without a loan.
I deserve to charge high-end for my intimate mastermind.
I have more than enough right now.

Training yourself to think in an abundance mindset is hard but inevitable if you wish to become wealthy. What you're thinking is what you're attracting. If you're thinking: *"Ugh, more bills to pay,"* guess what you're attracting more of?

The Universe is simple, it doesn't have any bias towards big or small purchases. It's meant to give you what you want. But if you're thinking about bills, and stressing about that constantly, think of the kind of energy you're sending out in the Universe. Because the Universe is mirroring it back to you. Train your mind to focus on positive wealth thoughts constantly. In this case, you do have to fake it till you make it. It's all about the stories and images you feed your mind.

If you're constantly Googling layoff news and reacting to LinkedIn posts of people complaining about getting laid off, you're sending off that energy to the Universe. You're now feeling stressed, thinking about your job security. The Universe responds to your thoughts and feelings constantly. And now you're sending a signal out to the universe about stress and layoffs. If you intentionally search and read stories of people who found jobs even during a difficult economic condition, guess what your mind will believe and what the

Universe will send you.

Close your eyes and think about what you most want right. Now remember what images, thoughts, stories you have been feeding yourself about it; and change the channel in your mind to mostly positive. You cannot control a negative thought that pops in. The key is to be aware of that thought and quickly change the channel in your mind to stories that actually serve you.

Avoid the Entrepreneurial Ostrich Syndrome

There is something I call the 'Entrepreneurial Ostrich Syndrome'. I completely made it up. It's when entrepreneurs start ignoring their money because it's too painful to look at it. I've been an ostrich a few times in business—busy hiding my head in the sand, rather than facing the numbers.

It's time to stop hiding from money. Stop ignoring your bills and taxes. Stop looking at credit card statements and paying them blindly, or worse, not paying them at all; or just paying the minimum balance and moving on. Stop ignoring your business's profit loss statement. Stop ignoring your sales and leads pipeline.

Don't hide. Face it. *Get comfortable with the discomfort of looking at your finances*

Play Money Games with the Universe

In fact, start enjoying looking at numbers. In Rhonda Byrne's incredible book, *The Secret,* she writes that when it comes to money, play games with yourself. Imagine your bills are actually you receiving cheques. Open those envelopes with excitement. Add a zero at the end, and imagine receiving this amount. Imagine receiving more and more such cheques. And say thank you to the Universe by closing your eyes when you receive such cheques. And that cheques are always greater than the bills. Be excited while paying taxes because more taxes mean you just made more money.

Thank Your Parents

I was five or six years old, when I was obsessed with a pink Barbie doll; with all of her necklaces and vanity mirror and hairbrush and all the accessories. Every time I spotted a Barbie, I wanted it with all my heart. I remember being at the mall one day, and saw a Barbie and asked my dad to get it for me. At that time, getting an expensive doll was simply out of the budget for him. So he said no, and I remember being heartbroken and crying for days. I remember being angry at my dad.

In another instance, when I was eight or nine years old, I remember walking into a bookstore with my parents. It was a fancy new Crossword store that had just opened in Ahmedabad. I walked in and chose an Astronomy book—it had a map of the night sky and contained information on all the constellations, planets, and stars we see in the night sky. I remember being so excited because I was obsessed with space and wanted to go to space someday. I showed it to my dad, expecting to be turned down again. To my surprise, he bought me the book, and two other books I wanted that day.

Our parents pay for us as long as they can, hoping we are capable of making our way into the world and standing on our own two feet. As children, sometimes we're hard on our parents. Some of us are extremely hard on our parents. It's time to let go. It's time to be grateful for everything that was 'paid for' for you.

Did your parents get you clothes, toothbrushes, diapers as a newborn?
Did they get you colouring books, story books and crayons to draw with?
Did you have a roof on your head?
Did you use electricity, water and other basic amenities?
Did they buy you school books, help you cover the books with brown paper and take you to school every day for years?
Did they take you to the dentist?
Did they host a few birthday parties for you, over the years?
Did they buy new clothes for you when you outgrew the old ones?
Did they take you to movies, to the circus, to concerts?
Did you learn a sport, or a hobby or a musical instrument?
Did you go on vacations every once in a while?

Did you get an education that helped you become independent?

Thinking about all the above, I have tears in my eyes because I remember how lucky my childhood and life has been. Sometimes we forget about the good things, and only remember being angry. Today, I urge you to thank your parents for everything they did for you.

It's one of the best ways to remove any money blocks. You're grateful and happy for everything you've received till you become self-dependent. Everything that someone else gave you and took care of for you. Even if you feel like it was too little, it was *their best* that they could do. I've noticed in my life that it's hard to attract more wealth and more money when we still think negatively about money. About everything we *don't have or didn't have* growing up. It's time to remove those blocks and be grateful from the bottom of your heart.

Write a message, or a handwritten note or tell them over a video call today just how much it means to you to have your parent's love and support. And how lucky you are that they paid for everything for you. It's also a game I play with the Universe: I list down things I'm grateful for every day. More specifically, I think about things I could enjoy because of the money I have today.

I've been known to receive unexpected money because I like to live in grateful energy. Surprise money has come in the form of tax refunds, a dividend cheque from my stock investments, a handful of course sales on a payment portal I wasn't even checking or promoting on, my investments generating multiple returns while I wasn't actively checking them, finding a better deal on a software subscription I was paying for, and receiving a gift from a loved one.

You can only manifest more of what you're grateful for already. *Attracting more money using gratitude is a wealthy move.*

Why YOU Should Make More Money

You have the seeds of wealth inside of you, you just need to nourish them and water them. The universe didn't make millionaires or billionaires any different. You have the same power within you as your inspiration.

I invite you to boldly journal right now and proclaim your reasons for making money. These are a few of mine:

Because $50,000 months are my minimum.
Because fuck patriarchy.
Because on rainy days you have money not just to survive, but to thrive.
Because I can pay for my future children's college education in cash.
Because I can hire the best people to help and support me at home and in my business.

Because life is uncertain and I always want to be able to live my best life.
Because I can take care of my parents and my sister.
Because I want to look and feel amazing.
Because Chanel and Cartier make us feel like a million bucks.
Because we cannot let trauma rule.
Because money in the hands of women can cause ripple effects for the whole world.
Because I'm here to put money into the hands of more women and men so they can do life-changing things.
Because I don't just want a seat at the table, I want the whole freakin' house.
Because how else am I going to empower my future daughter to be independent, if not by example.
Because earning millions a year is freaking badass and we got this.
Because Taylor Swift and other powerful women have shown us that it's safe to have money and be visible.
Because we need to be a powerful woman for our current family and to empower the next generation.
Because having more wealth is proof that I'm damn good at my job.

Homework: Journal It Out

What are your reasons for why you should make more money?

Name the people you're grateful for, who have helped pay for things in your journey. Send them a thank you message or call them today.

Start saying 'thank you' for every bill you pay, and for every service you use.

List down the money games you'll start playing with the Universe.

Chapter 9

Manifest Your Wealthy Life

When it comes to money, I am of the "make more, give more" mindset. As an Indian, and especially as a woman, it is taboo to talk about making money. If a woman talks about making more money, you get side-eye, but if a man talks about making more money, they're called ambitious.

Which is why, if you're a female founder, shout it out from the rooftops and share your victories—revenue, profits, and everything else. In fact, I noticed when I talked about money more often, my audience connected with me better, because I was sharing the raw real numbers of my business.

At this point, I don't have dreams of becoming a

billionaire or buying a jet plane. However, never say never.

But I do believe I'd like to have *enough* money to have the best of everything. If I go on a vacation, I'd like to stay in five-star resorts and get the best room with the best view, along with a private balcony and a private pool situation. I like to go to the best spa facility in the city because it relaxes me, helps me with better blood flow, relaxes my back muscles, and enables me to work better.

I like to purchase quality clothing items which cost more than fast fashion—which are highly unsustainable for our planet. I like to take care of my clothes and wear them for years and years. I like to purchase the best Macbook, iPhone and iPad so I can do my work well. I used my last iPad for six full years and then sold it in pristine condition to upgrade to the best iPad in the market now.

I've lived in Singapore for four years. Some time ago, my family visited me there; it was their very first international trip. It was a big milestone for us, and I was lucky enough to splurge on them. To pay for their flights, to show them around my favourite places and restaurants without looking at the cost, to do adventure sports and other activities as a family together, without worrying about anything. We went ziplining, bungee jumping, rode all the rides at Universal Studios, and went to all the best zoo experiences.

When you make more money, you can go beyond just taking care of your needs and wants, and splurge on your family experiences. I was able to help out my parents when I got married—I was able to share all wedding expenses equally.

I've been able to travel to 15 countries, and most of these were solo adventures. In the beginning, I couldn't afford the more comfortable resorts/hotels, so I did the best with what I had; I stayed in Airbnbs, hostels and cheap hotels. When I was younger, I had the hunger to experience new places and meet new people and I didn't let my budget stop me from traveling. Later, when my company started doing well financially, I splurged on five-star resorts for my solo trips and treated my husband to a vacation for his birthday.

Before I could purchase business class tickets, I spent hours in 30-hour-long economy flights to attend conferences, meet clients, network, and grow my business. I didn't own a single vehicle or property during most of my 20s, even though I could easily purchase them. I focused on growing my money by investing.

I have always believed that while I make my money, I need to pay it forward. I love giving money to charities and causes that feel close to my heart. With each passing year, I wish to make a bigger impact and I believe making more money will help me do it with ease.

I'm grateful for what I've been able to buy and

experience till now. I also have set my sights on what I want in the years to come—purchasing my dream home; having the ability to purchase a first-class ticket for my family without thinking twice; become a bestselling author and publish many more books; and become an angel investor for a couple of cool startups. All these dreams are a work in progress, while I hold gratitude for everything I've been lucky enough to do.

Upgrades are always available in all areas of life.

I've gone into upgrading the investments I make from public stocks to significant equity in private companies to investing in real estate with potential. I also keep upgrading the clientele I work with year on year. Being the youngest person, and sometimes, the only woman amid men in black suits and their black suitcases in the business class on flights makes me feel proud as well.

Upgrades are available in how I take care of my family, my team, my clients, and myself. All of this is possible for you. There is no unsafe vibe to it. There are no red flags to it. Us upgrading in all aspects of life hurts no one. *The Universe wants you to upgrade in all areas of life.* The Universe has no bias against me or you. The Universe is an ever-loving force of attraction that wants to see you happy and wants to see all your desires being met.

One of the ways I get into the right frequency is wealth affirmations to declare to the Universe what I'd like.

Make a Reservation with The Universe

As Rhonda Byrne advises in *The Secret,* make a reservation for your desires in advance. Just like when you book a hotel or a flight, you believe that hotel is already yours to enjoy in the future.

In the catalogue of the Universe, make your pick and make your booking. Is it a new car? Is it a new home in the best neighbourhood in the city? Is it reserving a spot for your kid in the best international school of your choice? Is it travelling to a country that you've always dreamed of?

Now imagine that the dream has already come true, and since you've made your reservation, it's already true in the invisible world and it's on the way to you in the physical world. Think the thoughts, feel the feelings, and send the love out into the Universe as though you have already received it. *Close your eyes for a minute and feel all the emotions of having received it.* Supply images, graphics, people, motions to that experience while you close your eyes. And see yourself already enjoying the thing that you used for.

Manifesting My Favourite Things in Life

I'm currently revisiting my childhood and early adulthood journals, starting from when I was around 12 years old up to my current age of 30. I have a deep love for journaling, so whenever you see me achieve something or realise one of my dreams—whether it's building a million-dollar business, being featured in *Forbes,* impacting thousands of clients, relocating to my dream country, or establishing the business and client base I now have—almost all of it, I mean literally all of it, I have visualized and written about multiple times in my journals.

I can see firsthand what can happen when you are truly dedicated to manifesting your dreams. Visualize, pour your heart into your journals, and outline the entire process. If you can journal daily, that's fantastic. However, even if you can't do it every day, use journaling as a tool to process your thoughts and visualize your goals.

I find nature to be the best background for visualization and gratitude. I love journaling and visualizing while I'm sitting on a beach in Goa, or while on a road trip in Iceland, or while breathing the fresh mountain air of Sidemen, Bali.

Write down five things you're grateful for, then list five things you're working towards and would like the universe's support with. Be as clear as possible. While it might take longer at times, it can also happen within a few short months.

I've written in my journal about owning multiple real estate properties in multiple countries, investing in amazing startups, and becoming an author. I have filled multiple journals throughout the years with these goals. It may seem like you're merely sending your thoughts out into the ether and that no one cares or is listening. Yet, energetically, you're affirming the importance of these desires to yourself. You're telling yourself and the Universe how much you want it.

Do you want it bad enough? Even if you don't believe in magic, God, or any other higher power, you should believe in your own energy and the intentions you are setting in the world. You possess incredible untapped power; much of the strength and magic within our souls, minds, and hearts remains untapped, probably about 90 per cent of it. Tapping into this energy involves bringing your deepest desires and thoughts to the surface, documenting them in your journal, and delving into them. But you should back up your intentions with action.

You need to be comfortable with calculated risks, making sure you're not acting impulsively. I remember when I manifested staying in a lovely resort from a hostel. I had just quit my software developer job and took two months off to travel and figure out my next action plan. The plan basically was to pay my bills and not go broke in a year. I booked a hostel in Bir, Himachal. The hostel was beautiful and nothing fancy. But as I was loitering around the beautiful village of Bir, I came across this beautiful boutique resort perched upon the mountain. I immediately felt like I had to stay there. I quickly Googled the hotel and it was 10 times what I was paying for the hostel. I had 12 months' worth of savings in my bank account and that was it. But I thought to myself, let's shoot my shot, what's the worst that can happen, somebody will reject my proposal—I could live with that. So I rang up the hotel, and luckily, the owner answered the call.

I explained that I had a small travel blog and would love to come stay for a day, experience their hotel and write about it on my blog. This was back in 2017, so influencer marketing wasn't as huge back then. To my disbelief, the owner said yes, and asked me to reach the hotel. I was shocked. I thought this was too real to be true. I was also scared a bit as to how easy this was. But the opportunity was too good to pass up.

So I lugged my backpack across the village and reached the hotel. The staff helped me check in, prepared special meals for me, even gave me a car with a driver to take me around the day. It was a Jeep which could go over rugged mountain roads with ease. I visited the nearby monasteries; watching Buddhist monks praying at sundown in the midst of the mountains is something I'll never ever forget. It was a beautiful two-night stay. I could see fireflies flying across the lawn at night, for the first time in my life. I met some cool people, had nice conversations. The hotel also had a horse manger and beautiful horses.

Another time, I manifested having the opportunity to invest in a cool company. I decided to diversify my investments. I was trading stocks in the public market and getting the hang of things there. But I thought the concept of angel investing was cool, and being from the tech world, (while I have no dreams of running my own tech company) I want to make meaningful investments in other SAAS (software as a service) companies. This is a story of how I manifested an investment which doubled in one short year.

I was traveling to Bali for my birthday. I was journaling by the river of a beautiful resort. I was also reading Tim Ferriss' blogs; even his old blogs from 2014-2015 are gold and still relevant today. In one of them, he was talking about his angel investing experiences. I already respected him a lot as an author and now I thought, I wanted to be an angel investor too.

It was time to level up my investing game. Note, that my biggest investments prior to that were my fixed deposits, which is not the smartest way to grow your money. So I wrote in my journal about it and visualized myself stepping into my role in this phase of life as not just a founder, but an investor empowering other founders and companies.

Three months after that day, I received an opportunity to invest in a Silicon Valley startup.

Sometimes, the Universe answers quickly. You just need to make your booking and announce exactly what you want. Sometimes, the Universe takes its own sweet time but I believe it's getting you ready to receive and maintain that desire for life. If you only take away one thing from this entire book, it's this: put it out there. Write about it in your journal, visualize it, and it will happen, sooner or later. Take your shot. Don't overthink yourself to death. Action is 100 times more valuable than overthinking.

I love imagining a BIG income number in my bank account. I'll copy a message from my bank transactions, paste it in my Notes app, and add a couple of zeroes to my credits. I'll put it up as a wallpaper on my phone till I truly get into the frequency and mindset and safety of receiving such big amounts being credited in my bank account. I have already manifested my love, my work and where I live. And have manifested my way out of tough situations. It works. I tell myself that I am freaking powerful. And everything I want will be mine, sooner or later.

Trusting myself is the biggest gift I give myself. I know that I love myself more than anyone else on earth. So, their opinions cannot be valued more than mine. I have a North Star for me, within me. I know what's best for me and I go out there and make moves to get it. *The Universe works with me to give me everything I desire, or better!*

I am closing my eyes and imagining 100 active clients inside my new mastermind program—104 to be precise, including my team. If the things that I wanted are yet to happen, I trust that I haven't yet become the version I need to create the magic, and sustain the magic. You give signals to the Universe. You give it the permission to give you the things you desire. But the wavelength of information that gets passed on to the Universe needs to be unwavering. We cannot keep changing these signals, wanting it badly one moment, and then thinking negative things about the thing we desire another moment. We control what we desire, we control putting the work in for what we desire, we control keeping the faith and intention for what we desire even if it seems like it's not working. But we do not control the timing of our desires.

Sometimes though, after experiencing trauma, pain or heartbreak, we stop trusting these same manifesting techniques that worked well for us. Our frequency changes to negativity. Healing trauma and pain is important. But know that you are still the same powerful manifesting force. And you can restart. You can trust yourself. You can attract anything you set your heart to. That's why that desire was put in your heart in the first place. The Universe isn't against our desires. The Universe wants to give us what we desire. But the when, and how needs to be surrendered. That's the Universe's problem—the *when* and *how* is none of your concern.

'This' or something better is my mantra.

The best way to release and surrender and get unattached to the desires and outcomes. If you have put an offer on your dream home, and it fell through, a better home is awaiting. If you are facing problems in your fertility and conception journey, your lovely baby is awaiting its perfect timing to meet you earthside. If you are waiting to land your dream client but the deal is stuck, the right set of deals is on its way to you. If your investment in a company fell through, another one with a better founder and performance is just around the corner.

I wouldn't have been able to do a lot of things if I always looked at money, specifically the lack of it, as a reason not to do things. I've always wanted to be well-traveled, so I made a list of new places I want to visit every year. How much do you want to bet I hit those lists every year? Because energetically, I proclaim my desires. And then, practically I make it happen. Except, of course, during the peak COVID-19 pandemic years of 2020-2021.

At the time of writing this, this year alone, in the past eight months, I've travelled to Sidemen, Phuket, Bintan, Iceland, Udaipur, Gujarat, Singapore and Malaysia. I've travelled almost every single month and I know whatever you manifest is possible for you as well.

This gives me goosebumps every time I think of it because I literally manifested my love, my partner, my future husband when I was just 17.

At 17, I prayed and hoped for a partner and the Universe listened to me. At the time, I felt very lonely as a teenager and felt like no-one understood me. In fact, the 11th and 12th grade were some of the darkest years of my life. We didn't have any classes in common or anything since he was senior to me. But I had observed him a couple of times in college playing volleyball and I thought he was so cute, and messaged him on Facebook. The rest, as they say, is history.

Let's talk about you. What qualities do you seek in a life partner? Put down non-negotiables for your future partner, so that you can know exactly what you're looking for.

I think my number one criteria was a kind heart. I think kindness is cool. I'm being brutally honest here—years of learning and living in the patriarchal world trained me to think I needed a rich man or the potential rich man to take care of me. That is a load of bullshit. And while there's nothing wrong in choosing a partner that is successful, what I'm saying is that shouldn't be the *only* criteria.

Become your own rich man.

You don't need any man to succeed in life. You need to trust yourself and your potential enough. At the same time, I would choose a partner that I can respect and believe in their potential. It's not a man or a woman thing, it's a respect thing.

If you can, marry your best friend. You can have fun

with each other, tell each other everything, and it's you and them against the world. That is very important. If it starts from friendship, then it's easy. This goes without saying but I think it still needs to be reiterated—choose a partner who doesn't abuse you in any way, emotionally, verbally or physically.

When you choose the right partner, they make your happy moment happier and make you feel on top of the world and support you and your goals and dreams. When you're going through bad days, they're standing with you like a rock, and that's amazing. My husband and I have been together for more than 14 years now. I do not believe in happily ever after, but what I do believe in is working on the relationship every single day to make it better and better, because finding a life partner is one of the biggest decisions you will ever make. So make it well.

Homework: Journal It Out

What are your favourite things that you're manifesting in your life right now?

In what ways, will you pamper your loved ones when you hit your next wealth milestone?

Today is the day you start trusting yourself fully, forever, irrevocably. Write down the reasons and show yourself evidence of why you are amazing.

Chapter 10

Building Your Wealth Affirmations

My mindset isn't always positive: I go through my fair share of 'down days.'

I journal a lot on days when I feel my mindset is getting affected by something. These affirmations are about money, success, health and relationships. Write your own version of it, believe it, visualize it, write it down daily in your money mindset journal. Read it, feel it, program your mind to believe it. I want to humbly note that mindlessly writing or repeating affirmations without being supported by relentless execution on your part is not going to be helpful.

Here are my go-to wealth affirmations:

I always have more money coming in than going out.

I always make at least $100K a month.

I have $1M in my bank account at all times.

People love paying me.

My work is of high value and worthy of massive compensation.

I have enough money to keep my family safe and secure. I also have enough money to spend for fun.

I love money, and money loves me.

I run a high-profit business.

Expenses low, revenue high is how I always run my business.

I save money with ease, and spend money with ease.

I love paying my team; it is amazing to pay people who support me.

I buy things without any guilt.

The more money I have, the more money I can use to

help others.

I am very comfortable having large sums of money, I am an excellent money manager and do great things with it.

I always have enough money for anything that I want to do in life.

I rise above the copycats and haters.

Life is happening for me, not to me.

Forgiveness is freedom to me.

I only attract soulmate customers who actually do the work and get results.

I always attract the right clients at the right time; great clients are attracted to me and there is never a shortage of them.

I am one of the smartest people in the world.

I feel confident and amazing while running my business.

I let go of any limiting beliefs, guilt and doubts about my ability to succeed in all areas of my life.

I choose to be successful in every area of my life—business, health, relationships and everything else.

I quickly learn the lessons that life teaches me via failures, setbacks and disappointments. I learn lessons quickly, and never repeat the same mistakes.

Freedom is my jam. I feel free to do whatever I want in all areas of life.

I feel at ease when I am in difficult situations and believe in my ability to figure things out and win.

I'm awesome at math.

I am intelligent and a quick-learner.

I'm good at tech, marketing, sales and copywriting.

My clients love me, my students love me.

I am always grateful for my blessings.

My work is necessary and revered by the world.

My clients are grateful I show up to work every day.

I control my peace, nothing and no one can take away my peace without my permission.

I prosper in health, I prosper in finances, I prosper in love, I prosper in peace and I am unstoppable.

I am free of the fear of rejection. Rejection is a necessary thing to achieve success. I act without fear of rejection. In fact, I'm always chasing fear because I know it will bring me to the next level of success.

I am smart, helpful and worthy.

I am kind, humble and here to serve.

I manage huge amounts of money with intelligence and tact.

I make money, I save money, I donate money, I use money to make my life and other people's life better.

I trust myself with money.

I am very proud to be free of judging other people and comparing them to myself.

I feel happy with my own achievements. I am strong-minded.

I am very proud to be free of imagining what others are thinking and saying about me. This freedom keeps me at peace, happy, successful and unleashed.

Each and every business call I make I start with an incredible level of positive expectation and prosperity.

I know that right now, somewhere someone's life is

better and more prosperous because of my products and services.

I love taking action. I love setting a goal, and working hard towards achieving it no matter what.

I love to close the client. When a client is closed, I rejoice knowing that my time has been well spent and I feel confident and excited about moving onto a new opportunity without wasting any time.

I grow personally and professionally every single day. I pursue growth. I am better today than yesterday. My only competition is me.

I am positive, strong minded and strong willed.

My positive affirmations, goal setting and constant action make me an incredibly successful businesswoman.

I love working out every day. I love my body in all seasons and love what it does for me. Moving my body, and sweating it out makes me feel good, and look good. I love endorphins. I love that working out decreases my stress and anxiety.

I love to meditate for 10 minutes every day. Meditating makes me feel calm, relaxed and grounded. Meditating helps me to handle the challenges of the day with a calm demeanour.

I attract success. It's easy to be successful. I rejoice in the fact that I am successful and will become more and more successful every day.

Success and good things are naturally attracted to me and I feel prosperous and amazing every day.

I feel grateful every morning when I wake up. I bounce out of bed first thing, knowing that the day is full of opportunity. I feel excited, confident and exhilarated each morning as soon as I open my eyes. My morning routine is sacred to me. I do it every single day to ground myself.

I am an excellent marketer, video creator, copywriter and business woman. I love creating content that helps people, changes their lives for the better and gives them tangible results.

Every piece of content I create helps someone grow and be better. This makes me feel powerful and happy and I absolutely love knowing that it guarantees further success for others and me.

I take action in my business to produce content because when people receive this information, positive transformation happens.

I am an awesome writer. Writing is fun and easy. My book will impact people all over the world, and help them improve their life.

I am a confident speaker. My speeches are interesting, fun and inspiring. My talks inspire people all over the world to take action and take control of their lives.

I love my husband. I love spending time with him. I feel at peace, relaxed and loved by him. We have so much fun together. I love discussing my goals and dreams, and us planning our dream life together.

I feel confident to talk to any successful person, business man, writer and speaker. They are just humans like anyone else. I feel confident to hold my steed and communicate with them easily.

I am a self-starter who does not need any external force to motivate me, all of my motivation comes from within and I can call on it at will.

I know that the habits I create will fuel me to work, when motivation doesn't show up.

I am a motivated and energetic person; I feel good every single day.

I am proud of myself and my success, I have achieved so much. And this is just the beginning. I feel humbled and honored.

I am a happy person who loves to live fully. I enjoy life and life is good to me. This makes me feel happy and exhilarated.

I love to travel and see new places. Being in nature grounds me. I take solace in the fact that nature is always available to me.

I am a powerful body, a powerful mind and a powerful soul. This makes me feel smart and deserving of the world's greatest levels of success.

My words are strong and powerful. They bring success to others when shared. I speak and write my words with conviction and confidence.

Homework: Journal It Out

It's your turn now.

Write down your favourite affirmations and put them up somewhere where you can see them daily. On your office desktop, on your mirror where you brush your teeth, on your kitchen fridge.

Which reservations are you making with the Universe today?

Chapter 11

From New Money to An Investor Mindset

It's quite crazy to think that until three years ago I had zero investments outside of fixed deposits. Fixed deposits growing at five-six percent growth rate were my go-to as I could invest there without the fear of losing my money and thinking too much. I just focused on making money rather than investing it.

I soon realized that making money and investing your money are two *different* skill sets. Both are equally important. In fact, you'd argue the latter is more important. If you don't learn how to grow your money so it can beat inflation every year, your capital is shrinking instead of growing and that's just not the vibe. I started making investments starting with very small amounts, and eventually investing larger chunks of money, which felt scary sometimes.

I started with the Indian public stock market, sought the help of my family members who knew much more about it than I did. If you don't have access to a family member or a friend, make YouTube your best friend or hire a financial planner. It's easy to invest in the public stock market because it doesn't take a huge amount for you.

In time, I started investing in the US public stock markets too. That was a significant amount of money compared to what I had spent so far in the Indian stock market. However, I chose to invest in the top 10 companies of the world—companies whose products I use on a daily basis and that portray strong technical charts—so I felt a certain kind of security and peace of mind.

I was reading Tim Ferriss' blog on angel investments, and while journaling I really made it known to the Universe that I would be available for investing in the right companies privately.

On top of being a 100 percent owner in my own company, I wanted to diversify. Naval Ravikant says the only way to grow wealth is by owning a company or owning equity in a company. I wanted to do both. A few months after that journal entry, an opportunity presented itself. I invested a significant amount of money in a software company started by my mentor at the time.

The opportunity was available to only a few people at the time and I truly felt like my journaling desires were answered. At that time, it felt risky to invest that amount—angel investments fail 99 percent of the time. Angel investments can amount to your seed investment going to zero, or it hits the sky. But I trusted my gut and thought either way I'd have data and learnings to rely on for my future investments and made it happen. At the time of writing this, my investment has already doubled within a little more than a year, at least on paper.

At 28, I didn't own a car or any real estate. I still don't own a car as I see no need for it. But I invested in an apartment in my hometown in an upcoming neighbourhood. At the time of writing this, the market rates have significantly gone up in comparison to when I purchased the apartment. Apparently, a big Bollywood celebrity also purchased an apartment right near mine. That's good news to me! I'm looking forward to a nice rental cheque every month when it's all ready to operate. Purchasing a property is simply converting your paper bills or a number in your bank account into a physical entity. You now own something solid.

I hold the vibe of trusting my gut, listening to smart people around me, and holding the energy that all my investments are going to go up and up and up. Of course, there will be economic downturns, Act of God, or things beyond my control. But I believe overall, it will be a net positive.

And if I lose money on certain investments, I trust myself to make it back from my main company and my other investments. There are times when my business was slow, my investments were flourishing and I was able to pay my bills and live a good life without stressing.

What if I asked you to trust:

Trust that all your real estate investments will be attracting the best renters, and the neighbourhood will flourish, and your property rates will go up and up and up.

Trust that while you cannot control the stock market, that your chosen stocks will overall continue to go up and will keep paying you nice dividends.

Trust that your angel investments, while risky, don't have to feel like that, and you can do your due diligence, and trust that one or two right investments can make up for the rest of the duds.

Trust that you cannot fuck this up because what doesn't go your way either makes for a good story or a good lesson for next time.

Trust yourself that you are making wealthy moves on a daily basis. Every time I fear letting go of a large sum of money, whether it's for stocks, angel investing or making a huge down payment on a property, I trust myself to replenish it and make more.

I trust that it's all working in my favour. I tell myself it's safe to invest in modes that grow my wealth. I tell myself that it's the wealthy move required at this time to ensure my and my family's future is secure and thriving.

During the COVID-19 pandemic, many businesses suffered. Online businesses like mine flourished because online education and learning exploded, which was a great time to make money. As the world returned to normal (and thankfully so) people's needs changed and the online business saw a drop compared to the pandemic years.

I could've beat myself up about why the business dipped, and if I could have done something more to bring it back to the 2020-21 level. But I focused on leveraging the capital I did have and put it to work in different avenues. Since I was doing everything I could to grow my company, I thought, how else can I grow my money? Well, let's look into investing. There's always a solution, a creative solution for when you feel like you've hit a dead-end.

Running my business for over eight years now, I know that there are some times in business when you are in the "wait it out" or "survival" phase because of internal or external conditions. The growth of a company doesn't just go up and up and up every month. This is, in fact, true for your favourite public companies such as Apple, Google, Nvidia as well. and I invite you to check out their technical charts over the last few decades, and normalize that it is not a growth curve to infinity. Wealthy moves include developing the skill set to make your money and to invest your money. Both are important!

I invite you to release any limiting beliefs you might have about money or investing:

"I've always sucked at math."
"I'm bad with numbers."
"I'm not good at investing."

Start now—don't wait till you feel like you are ready. Save a portion of your monthly income and leverage it somewhere it will grow faster. You don't have to wait till the perfect time or the perfect opportunity or the perfect economic conditions. Today is the day to start making those wealthy moves, baby!

My investing journey started in my 20s. I have to admit, I feel like I started investing a bit late so I wish I could have started earlier. But my intention is to share what worked for me so that hopefully it would help you become a savvy investor. Remember, making money is ONE skill. Growing money is ANOTHER skill. You want to make your money work for yourself, otherwise inflation will eat it up. If you have a million dollars in the bank right now, 20 years down the line, it will shrink if it sits there, doing nothing.

The 50-30-20 Breakdown for Investing:

Allocate 50 per cent of your earnings towards saving and investing, ensuring you're being frugal and investing smartly. Devote 30 per cent to essential expenses, covering your day-to-day needs. Finally, reserve 20 per cent for leisure and enjoyment, enhancing your overall quality of life. It's important to note that these calculations are exclusive of taxes.

Let us suppose you earn $10,000 per month. After accounting for a 20 per cent tax deduction, your take-home income would be $8,000. Following the rule, allocate $4,000 to savings, $2,400 to expenses, and the remaining $1,600 for leisure activities.

Reframing Taxes and Expenses

If you've heard your parents or grandparents talk about how taxes suck, you're not alone. This means you probably have negative thoughts around taxation. You can choose to believe what society tells you about taxes or you can turn around the situation into a mindset that supports you and your wealth goals.

While I don't support any political parties and rarely foray into sharing my political views, taxes are an important backbone of the country. It's how we get water and electricity and roads and safety and schools and malls and general sense of human lifestyle. And while you should work to minimize taxes via all legally available methods, know that wealthy people pay a lot of taxes. Though a huge chunk of money leaving your account sucks, you have created a positive dent in the economy. You created a lot of activity in the economy, a lot of transactions to now be able to pay taxes. The more money you make, the more taxes you'll pay. It's a good problem to have.

My best year in business, my company made a lot of revenue—I had a hefty tax bill to pay. I was complaining to my accountant and he told me, *"Roota, more taxes mean you're making more. You're in a higher tax bracket than most people which means you're making more than most people. It's a good thing, because you also get to keep more."*

Wealthy people pay an insane amount of taxes. They pay more taxes in a month than most people make in a year. And that's completely alright. You should celebrate every time you pay taxes and upgrade to the next tax level.

It is a privilege to pay taxes on your employee's behalf.
It is a privilege to pay GST on the goods sold.
It is a privilege to pay corporate tax on the profits your company made.
It is a privilege to pay personal tax on the salary your company gave you.
It means you're a badass and you're a boss!

Taxes need to be paid either way. It's best if you change

your vibe and pay them with joy rather than frustration. On any given day, you're always spending money. You buy a coffee, you hail a cab, you order food delivery, you pay your phone bills, you purchase groceries. On certain days, you spend on a gorgeous date night, or buy a birthday gift for your loved one, or book flights to your next adventure, or purchase a new device or purchase new clothes that make you feel fabulous.

It takes money to survive and thrive. We're spending our money with multiple different businesses on a single day. These businesses are thriving because of our spending. How would it feel to visualize the same energy for our business?

I tell myself:

People love purchasing my courses and digital products every day.
People love spending on my books and journals and audiobooks.
People love purchasing my mastermind to level up their game.
People love to hire me for 1:1 coaching and consulting.

If people can't make a purchase immediately, my free content serves them and they are inspired to save up for my offers and then purchase.

Our job is to worry about creating great products as creators and entrepreneurs.

Our job is not to worry about how other grown adults will afford our programs. No-one is forcing anyone to make purchases. *We need to trust our clients and just help them make an informed decision.* How? With your content, your videos, your emails, your sales calls.

There was a point when I used to think $10,000 months was a big deal. It took me four years to get to that point. I used to dream about it and write about it in my journal every day. So much so that it hurt when every single month for those four years I didn't hit my goal. And then a month later, I did. And then, $10,000 months felt like nothing. At this point, my company has generated at least $10,000 per month for the last five years in business. Mostly much more with the highest month being $88,000 per month. And then I realized, *you have to make it not a big deal.*

Let's say $10,000 per month is your dream income. It's not a big deal. Release the craziness around the number. Release the overwhelm around the number. Know that there are a ton of millionaires and billionaires for whom $10,000 every month is not life-changing money. For you to achieve that, you have to feel the same way.

Currently, I'm holding the same vibe for hitting $100,000 months in my company. The same principle applies for your dream monthly income. I know sometimes people operate from the mindset of finding the cheapest option to get something done. As someone who comes from a middle-class family, I get it. I truly do. In business, some people go extra crazy and hunt for deals and coupon codes; choose the cheapest software tool or hire the cheapest freelancer; or buy the cheapest course to learn something. I know for me, how I do one thing is how I do everything. I like to invest in resources, both technology and people, that are going to help me show up in the best way for my business.

Over the years, I've seen the mindset shift in my clients where they realize this; when they purchase their first MacBook, they celebrate in our client community. Or when they purchased a professional quality microphone, or got a real camera to show up for their brand with confidence; to when they hired their very first real team member, and walked away from a freelancer mindset and entered their entrepreneurial era. I love celebrating these wins with them.

I have also invested in mentors over the years. In some cases, I definitely could not afford their price point but I knew to enter the next level of business, I needed to learn from the best; this meant I needed to leave my comfort zone financially as well. I trust myself to make smart decisions about investing my money in the right resources and mentors at any point.

There were times where it made no logical sense to invest an amount in the mentorship but whenever I've intentionally made an investment, it has paid off multiple times in the best way. In terms of business numbers, skills, networking, community, opportunities, mindset and so much more. It has always opened my worldview and mind and pushed me out of my own bubble.

There was a time when I decided that I needed to level up, and I chose a mentor to work with. It cost $36,000 per year to invest in their business mastermind and it was the most significant investment I had ever made. At the time, my business was going through a slump, and I was barely covering bills, team expenses, and salaries. As a small business owner, some months are more challenging than others. Despite the uncertainty, I committed a $15,000 down payment to join a mastermind program. It turned out to be life-changing. The return on investment was at least five times in a short period, and multiples times over in the long term. This decision not only enhanced my skills but also made me trust my decision-making abilities and mental frameworks.

I know investing in personal growth can be difficult, especially when it involves tangible resources like money. Give it your all and make it work. I've invested over $100,000 in coaching, personal development, books, conferences, courses, and masterminds. The result? I'm a more confident, self-assured, and stable person. Trust yourself, invest in yourself, and remember that money can be replenished. *And the greatest wealthy move is investing in yourself.*

Homework: Create A Game Plan and Start Executing

Which investing container are you going to start learning more about and start activity investing in?

Which lies are no longer serving you about investing, saving, debt, taxes and expenses?

It's not too late to start. You don't need to start big. You can start saving and investing with whatever your current financial situation is. It's about building the right investing muscles that will serve you as you keep climbing your wealth milestones.

Chapter 12

You Are An Artist

When we were children, I think a lot of us were encouraged by our parents to pursue art and a world outside of studies. Weirdly, as we grow up, a career in the arts is looked down upon by the society, and thought of as a non-lucrative option in comparison to Science, Tech, Engineering and Mathematics (STEM) careers.

I'm grateful that my parents encouraged me to read books when I was at school. My mom used to pick me up from school at 4 pm every day, and every few days we used to march straight towards the library, to borrow a couple of books. Library day was what I looked forward to the most, because I had gobbled up all the books in the past couple weeks, and now could spend hours looking for my next set of books to devour.

I dove deep into the worlds of *Agatha Christie, Nancy Drew, The Famous Five, Sherlock Holmes,* and saw myself in them. I could disappear into a book, and life would become an adventure instead of just surviving the monotony of school, studies and sports. Reading inspired me to start writing. I wasn't writing novels or short stories or anything. I started journaling a lot, about my day, about my friends, about my crushes at school. I couldn't share everything with my parents, so obviously all the tea—ha!—had to go somewhere. Those journals helped me a lot and that was the art I created for myself.

I was also encouraged to go to drawing classes, which honestly was a bit annoying at first. I wasn't good at drawing, and I had no interest in drawing flower pots and vessels and stuff. All I wanted to do was draw paintings at my own will, without any rules. This motivated me to come home and practice and draw whatever I wanted. That was another way I created art, for myself, just for the sake of it.

Over nine years of running my company and I realized that if you worry about the business a lot, things tend to get worse. But if you have fun, treat it as art, enjoy writing emails, writing ad copies, creating ad creatives, shooting videos, and treat them as creating something meaningful from absolutely nothing, it adds so much joy to the day.

And at the end of the day, regardless of the numbers, you

feel fulfilled and sleep better. Whatever you're sharing with the world today—media, code or anything—it's a piece of art. It's something you created out of nothing, and it deserves love, importance and respect. And it needs to be seen by the world.

"Do not let anything stop you from making art. Just make things. Do not get so caught in this (negativity) that it stops you from making art. Or if you need to, make art about this (negativity). But never stop making things." That's Taylor Swift during her Apple Music interview, while she was promoting one of her recent albums.

I identify more as an artist rather than an entrepreneur or writer because every video I create is a piece of art. Every lecture and training I create as a coach is a piece of art. Every chapter I write as a writer is a piece of art. Art makes the world beautiful, and art makes you feel alive. Art makes you feel something—all the sadness, tears, growth, frustration, trauma, and healing. It's such a human part of the experience.

When I see many people on social media worrying about how Artificial Intelligence (AI) will take over their jobs and how humans won't be needed anymore, I think AI will make our lives easier and smarter, reducing the kind of labour needed to do different tasks. It will free up our time and creativity to produce more art.

Taylor Swift is an incredible songwriter. She has written

hundreds of songs based on heartbreak, personal experiences, trauma, and people taking advantage of her work. There's no other Taylor Swift in the world. I cannot produce a Taylor Swift song. We cannot all gather in an 80,000-capacity stadium, sing her songs, and feel the intensity of that beautiful human experience anywhere else but a Taylor Swift concert.

In the words of Rumi the poet, art touches your heart and makes you feel something, makes you cry. It's because you are a human going through your experiences. When you create art, keeping that human experience in mind, not being a capitalist, not thinking you are better than everyone else, but sharing your humanity, vulnerability, creativity, and art for the betterment of the world, so that people can feel better, learn better, grow better, and heal better—that is the best thing you could ever do to make the world a better place.

If you're a coach or a teacher, your lectures, trainings, and videos have the power to change someone's life for the better—for them to learn skills, gain confidence, and become more than they are now, to create a better life for themselves. And that is art. You should create it with the mindset of being grateful for the opportunity to create this piece of art, not with the thought of it being a mere task.

Certain movies make our hearts cry, while hard-hitting documentaries drive hundreds of thousands of dollars towards donations. For instance, I watched a Netflix documentary called Chasing Coral, about coral reefs and their impact on the environment, and it led me to donate to their cause through the WILD Foundation, which helps sea creatures. Documentaries on subjects like sex trafficking, earthquakes, and other challenges evoke emotions and drive you to take action. It makes you sad and frustrated, but it also motivates you to take action to make things better in your control. How beautiful is that?

I believe every one of us is an artist, with art bubbling inside us. It is teeming to be let out and put out into the world. We often get caught up in competition and the fight for space. However, each of us has an equal space and an artistic contribution to provide to the world.

There are no accidents in the universe. Every one of us was born on Earth to produce something, to create art. I have written this book on my phone, iPad, laptop and journals. While on international planes smooshed in my economy seats, in transatlantic business class flights, in the public transport, in the park, in coffee shops across Singapore, by the beach, in beautiful five-star resorts, in my parent's home in the room I grew up in, at my in-law's place, in car rides, while business was doing well and even while I felt like everything was crumbling to the ground.

The skill to write, to express emotions, to express imperfections, to share a story to move hearts has been the most rewarding journey. Reading and writing is how I make sense of the world. They say if you can write it and explain it, you've really understood it. I've written countless emails, social media posts and stories, hundreds of sales pages and sales emails—and writing is literally responsible for any success I've had to date.

Pain makes you write deeper and more authentically. I had this mindset that I will write only when things are going well. Firstly, *going well* is a vague definition. And as someone who tries a million things, tests a dozen things at a time, and has many hot irons in the fire, things are never quite perfect or going well.

Use the pain to create art. Or the pain eats you up. Use the pain to write deeply, to share your raw vulnerable stories, to create paintings and sculptures and write code and write books. It is a superpower to *feel this deeply* about something. If you're feeling it, a fraction of 8 billion people in the world are also feeling it. And they need your creation and art to heal, to progress, to succeed. Do not take your pain lightly, use it. *Your art is a wealthy move.*

Take An Artist Trip

The Artist's Way: A Spiritual Path to Higher Creativity by Julia Cameron is one of my favourite books of all time. In it, she mentions a concept called "Artist dates"—and I want to offer you an extended concept called 'Artist trips.'

At the time of writing this, I'm in Sidemen, Bali, working on this chapter. And while I can write at home and I do write in cafes, my balcony etc., sometimes that familiar environment stifles my creativity. On top of that, I run a full-blown company so the pressures and responsibilities and putting out fires part of my CEO job always takes priority over creative endeavors that I want to pursue like writing this book. I don't get my best ideas sitting at my office desk, so changing up the environment is important.

We are set in our habits and patterns and similar brain neurons firing when we are in our comfortable environment like our home. So, I challenge myself to get out, pick out a lovely hotel in a brand-new unknown place I've never been to, hyper-focused and hyper-fixated on one creative project with zero distractions from the outside world. I've done this multiple times in the past few years.

I went to Bir Billing, Himachal Pradesh, when I had just quit my job to work out my next move.

I went to Cambodia to plan out my very first digital program.

I visited Jaipur, India and lived in the palace city while I aggressively filmed Marketing Accelerator 2.0 which went on to have 2,200 clients and a million dollars in sales. I was in my head about this project, I knew the stakes were high, so I was heavily procrastinating on recording the modules of this program even though the deadline was looming. I knew I had to physically move to a location that would inspire me.

Artist trips saved me, and I ordered room service all day across four days and got the beast done. I went to a Singapore beach resort while recording the modules of my Vortex Mastermind. Whenever I create programs, it's typically a four-six-month-long ordeal so it's common for me to feel exhausted from conceiving and creating the project. Artist trips help me breathe new life into my efforts, and the access to nature rejuvenates me and keeps my spirits high.

Your bad habits and bad patterns from your home do not have to follow you. You can easily break habits in new environments. For example, I'm waking up three hours earlier than I did at home because I'm inspired and I want to get on with my day. I'm hoping to take this habit with me back home.

I love doing artist trips within the country I live and abroad. Do whatever feels good to you. This doesn't need to be a fancy trip where you need to spend a lot of money. I love figuring out the food, groceries, transportation to new places I got to. Talking to locals and figuring out their stories. I recommend taking artist trips solo. When you travel solo, other travellers also love talking to you; I noticed when I'm travelling with my partner or in a group, people don't talk to you much.

I recommend not booking a lot of things and not creating itineraries of 10 things to visit when you're there. You should explore and travel and see a couple of awesome places to spike your inspiration and creativity. But keep it open for serendipity and free will because you're there to work on your art.

Your next book
Your next program
Your next app
Your next software
Your next music album
Your next movie idea
Your next research paper
Your next game plan

I came upon this idea of the Artist trips while I was driving my scooter with the perfume of impending rains blessing me, and all I could see was neon green rice paddies, nestled in front of the mountains as far as the eye can see. I rented a scooter, added a litre of petrol that will ensure I can drive to a nearby waterfall hike and back, drove for an hour, and it was meditative. Your best ideas come when you're in a flow.

I hiked up to the top of the mountain, got a few more ideas along the way, and jotted down in my journal which I always carry wherever I go. I drove back to my resort. I had a nice swim in the pool while it was raining; then I checked in with my parents. This day led to me writing 3,000 words in a day and planning my next few chapters, when the most I could do at home was 700 words a day.

Right now, as I present this idea to you, you are already thinking of reasons you cannot do artist trips. Maybe because of kids or loved ones not supportive or work or whatever.

Do it anyway. There's nothing such as perfect timing. Your dreams deserve it. Your art deserves it.

Sowing Season vs Harvesting Season

I'm writing this part of the chapter by a gurgling river, with cool water nestling across the view of the grand Mt Agung, the biggest active volcano in Indonesia.
Sometimes we feel like we need to know the full map before we start walking towards our goal. That's not true. If we stop and do-nothing and whine and complain that the path is dark. We know nothing.

But if we take a step ahead and self-lead ourselves, it's like we are lighting a candle. Even when you light a candle you cannot see the full path but you know the next five steps in front of you. And as you keep asking, the path keeps on illuminating.

For example, currently after running and growing my company for seven years, I feel depleted. It feels like I have run out of answers. It feels like someone changed the test questions on the topics I studied for and flipped them. The only common denominator in life, and more so in entrepreneurship, is change. It's not the first time I've felt this way. But this time, it feels different. I feel lost. The company I want to create and how I want to do it. Logically, you look at the industry and see what's working and model on that, you do an in-depth competitor analysis or you hire a consultant/ coach to guide you. I've done all that at certain times in this journey.

But now, I'm out of it. I don't think anyone I see is running the kind of business I wish to run. I'm scared of doing things my way, just because that's not how other people do it. No matter how strong I am, sometimes I too fear the judgement of people. What if I do something my way and I fail, and all the world gets to see?

I know this book is about advice that has personally helped me. But this section doesn't have a conclusion. We work through things. Things are a work in progress. Currently I'm pondering over what's my next step. When that's decided, I'll light that candle and the rest of the path will slowly illuminate.

But before that, I need to know where I'm going. Where I wish to go, and not what the news, media, family, competitive research, mentors tell me to go. That requires thought, and that takes time. Come to think of it, at the end of the day, *wouldn't you want to have earned it anyway? Do we really value things that come easily to us and land in our laps?* That's why most lottery winners lose it all…because their mindset cannot comprehend how they got it all. They don't have the strength, tenacity, resilience, and the character of steel to maintain it. If we want something lasting, it takes time. It's incredibly hard. It's worth the wait.

There are some harvesting/reaping seasons and some sowing seasons. You cannot always be reaping, you need to take time to make the soil fertile again, think and then sow. And creativity needs space, patience, thinking time and to not chase behind reaping always. Sometimes, the wealthy move is taking our time to think, move in silence, regroup your priorities and to stop chasing goals mindlessly.

Homework: Journal It Out

Which activities do you do in your career that you can reframe as creating art? How will it add more joy and fulfillment to your day?

What big project have you been sitting on because of fear or judgement or just lack of bandwidth? Plan an artist trip over the next couple months and get a move on it.

Recognize whether you are currently in sowing or harvesting season. Both seasons are of equal importance. Be peaceful if you are in sowing season, make moves, move in silence, get ready for a big payout (harvest) later.

Chapter 13

30 Things I Wish I'd Known Before 30

I wish someone had told me these things when I was a 20-year-old figuring out life by myself. I didn't have a lot of women to look up to in my life and I thought as your big sis, I'll share the advice I wish I had been given, especially about life and business. I've learned a lot while travelling around the world, meeting people, attending the best conferences, designing my own courses, programs and masterminds and I want to share that with you. Again, take everything with a grain of salt. Use what you need, discard the rest.

1. Nothing shows people's true colours than adversity.

2. "Money only solves money problems" – Naval Ravikant, *The Almanack of Naval Ravikant*

3. There are too many rich, unhappy people. Strive not to be one of them.

4. Copycats will always play catch up. Put your head down and keep walking forward.

5. "The race is not to be won, it's to be run" – Ruskin Bond, *How To Live Your Life*

6. Be kind. Kindness is cool.

7. Make money. Loads of it. And help others with it.

8. 1 percent improvement daily is the goal. It's You Vs You.

9. The greatest pieces of art in the world—Leonardo da Vinci's Mona Lisa, Taylor Swift's albums, your favourite book—are a product of labour, of pain, for extended amounts of time. Nothing is an overnight creation.

10. Social media makes us dopamine addicts. Recognize it and use it accordingly, sparingly. Don't let it use you.

11. The best life is a life lived offline, rather than showing people online how good your life is.

12. Accept that the first draft of anything will be shitty. Mastery comes from iteration.

13. Everything starts with you believing. If you believe your work is important, and show up in that way, people will respond to it in the same way.

14. We cannot count how many weeks we have left with our parents. Make the best of each one.

15. Crying is cathartic and healing. Sometimes, you just need to play a sad song or watch a sad movie and cry it out.

16. It's harder to keep going than it is to give up. It's harder to choose kindness, than to be hurtful. Choose the hard thing. *"We can do hard things." –Glennon Doyle*

17. Stop yourself enough to take rest, to go on that trip with your best friend even though you have a new family now, go take that Master's degree even if you're 50, reach out to that estranged cousin and make new memories. Life is too short.

18. Rest is productive. Period. Fuck you, hustle culture.

19. Taking walks outside is guaranteed to clear your head and turn you into an idea machine.

20. Marriage is hard. Don't believe the PDA-inflicting couples on social media who make it look easy. A good marriage (in my opinion) is epic, and fun and disappointing and annoying and heart-wrenching—

all in one.

21. Keep it simple. Whatever you are currently overthinking about and overwhelmed about, it can be simplified—I guarantee you.

22. Beware of those people who spend all their time showing you their perfect life on social media or otherwise.

23. Comparing yourself to others never helps. Stop comparing your existence to hundreds of people's highlights on social media. Love yourself enough to not do that.

24. Sometimes, it's okay to give it all up for the sake of our health, mental and physical. It's truly irreplaceable.

25. Friends who secretly take joy in your downfall, avoid them. Life's too short to keep friendships going when you have clearly outgrown each other.

26. Your in-laws are not horrible by default. Yes, some in-laws, just like some people, are horrible. Don't automatically buy into the narrative. You can lead yourself to create a beautiful relationship.

27. Trauma can be the best teacher, as long as you learn how to harness it.

28. Smoking is not cool. Drinking too much alcohol is not cool. Doing hard drugs is not cool.

29. Find things that light you up: your favorite city to enjoy the rain in, your favourite musical artist, your favourite author, your favourite movies and enjoy them frequently without guilt.

30. Profit and cashflow is queen. Not revenue!

Homework

If you're liking this book so far, would you do me a favour and share it with three of your friends? Gift them this book or simply tell them how this book helped you—it would make me the happiest.

And here's another shameless plug: go to my website *www.learnwithroota.com* and find out more about my digital products, courses and masterminds so you can start getting the practical skills to support you in your wealthy moves journey. My mastermind helps you with my personal mentorship and accountability on a daily basis, and I would love to help you get to your next level in business!

Chapter 14

When You Feel Like It's Not Working Out

These are words I want you to read when the ground feels shaky, when you feel like nothing's working out and when you're looking for inspiration, and hope that it's all working out in your favour.

Finding Gratitude Daily

As I write this, I'm sitting at a resort in Sidemen, Bali, staring at the gurgling river, the mountains and it's so peaceful. A lovely hostess comes and asks for my breakfast order. I order pancakes, coffee, fruits and keep staring at the green expanse in front of me. The view is so beautiful, but my mind feels heavy and I feel beaten down.

This past month was incredibly hectic with work and travel. My company has been trying to close some client deals which seem to be in limbo. It's hard to not take sales rejections personally. I keep telling my clients this, but of course, it's tough. On top of that, a request for a loan deal that I need to make an investment, has been stuck for weeks and it makes me doubt myself. My self-worth majorly comes from the amount of money I make or how successful my company is. I obviously don't recommend this, and this is something that I am working on.

I decided to take out my journal. I began writing out a list of everything cool and amazing that had happened to me this month. Before I started, I thought all of it had sucked and I was worthless and my list would come up empty. I needn't have thought that, because here are 10 things that happened that I was incredibly grateful for and proud of having done.

1. I hosted our first company team retreat after working remotely for seven years.

2. I hosted our first ever in-person meetup so we can connect deeper with our clients and community.

3. I went on my first solo international trip to Bali after three years, and a solo trip in Goa (I hadn't travelled solo in a while because of the pandemic).

4. Sometimes, I don't believe what I have done to

deserve the unconditional love of my partner, Rachit, and the ways in which he supports me and my dreams.

5. I reserved my first-ever real estate property which is beginning to look like a very smart investment decision.

6. We had 'soulmate' clients renewing for another year into our mastermind. Soulmate clients who listen to my advice, put in the damn work, and don't give up even when the going gets tough. Instead, they come on coaching calls and ask for help. I really love working with resilient clients who can dust themselves and pick themselves up.

7. I did a live masterclass which I gave my all to—and the attendees had massive breakthroughs.

8. I finally began to grow a slightly active community in Singapore after two years of feeling a bit lonely as an expat.

9. I worked on optimizing a team, even though a long-time team member was leaving. This became an opportunity to hire another member who currently fits our company needs.

10. I'm finally writing this book, even though there are 100 things I need to do for work.

Why am I telling you all this? It's because at any point in time, your life will never be 100 percent perfect. Human life is 90 percent suffering and 10 percent worth living, I joke to myself often. But can we shift the focus to the things that we can be grateful about right now? Maybe you are struggling in a relationship right now, but your health is doing great and you're working out daily. Or maybe your career is on the rise and you're proud of it, but you rarely have time for social activities. A 100 percent satisfied human never exists, and pain is a part of it.

Suffering is a choice though.

I promise you, anyone you look up to, be it your mentor or your favourite influencer or your favourite hero, they are going through the same thing as you. If you don't feel great right now, I request you to open a physical notebook, grab a pen and jot down the things you are grateful for, as recently as last month. Be as specific as possible instead of just saying "my health" or "my marriage" or "my parents". If your work is that of a coach or mentor or guide, maybe you're currently going through what you are going through, because someone, someday, will go through the exact same thing, and you can help them through this.

Only when we are suffering, do we learn to appreciate joy.

Only when we have lived through the night, do we

appreciate the morning.

Only when we have lived through weakness and fear, do we have stories of heroism and survival to share.

Only when a mother labours through the night, do we have a new life to celebrate and cherish.

Only when two lovers are pulled apart, do they cherish what they had.

Only when your knees start cracking, you realize the importance of movement and youth.

Choose to be grateful—every single day.

Don't Believe Your Hype—and Don't Believe Your Haters

There was one particular time (among many) when I was convinced that my business was on the verge of closure.

I had started promoting my signature program on social media with ads that were being watched by hundreds of thousands of people all across the country. Since I had worked hard to create a program that helped people be successful freelancers, full of all my wisdom and expertise bundled up into the course, along with our coaching, I thought people would be eager to go through our free resources and invest in the program.

Oh boy, was I wrong!

I thought I would see an outpouring of love because in India, freelancers were finally getting a blueprint from someone who scaled a freelancing business, and could now guide and mentor them. And yes, a few people did think that and invested in my program. But I also got a storm of negative comments. Haters and trolls were having a ball of a time commenting hateful, sexist, negative things about everything—how my program was a scam, my looks, my accent, how I should stop doing what was I doing and start a makeup business (some comments said that because I had makeup on in my ad videos, it is all I'm good at) and even the shape of my eyebrows. Yup, people couldn't even leave my eyebrows alone. Because in this day and age, how can a woman be good at anything other than something related to her looks?

Some of the messages were so mean, I would cry for hours in front of my partner. He did everything to knock some sense into me, saying how these people didn't have anything better to do in their lives. I couldn't understand why everyone was hating on me, when I was just trying to run my business and help people. I would wake up, check some ad comments, go into a spiral, and take the rest of the day off. Clearly, it was not the most productive time for my business.

Since my ads were visible to everyone, people were taking advantage of my program, including threatening to pirate my content which I had worked so hard to produce. This was not good for my mental health. I began hating my business. I didn't want to help people or make money from my business anymore; all I wanted to do was lie in my bed and cry all day.

Then, one day, I happened to be scrolling Facebook and came across a post by its founder, Mark Zuckerberg. He'd written about a charity he recently supported, and under that post were some of the meanest and most offensive comments on Earth. Someone who created the platform that changed the face of social media in the history of the world was not spared the spiteful or mocking remarks of people online. That changed something in me.

Why the hell was I letting a bunch of strangers on the internet dictate my mood? Why was I so ready to shut down my business after being hit with a few negative comments and trolls? Why was I paying any heed to people who were just jealous of the people actually working on their dreams? Why was I torturing myself over what some faceless, follower-less troll accounts had to say about me and my expertise? I had a major shift in my mindset and I asked myself: *"What can I learn from this? What is life trying to teach me with this?"* I strongly believe, *"In life, everything is happening for us and not to us."*

Not all comments were hateful or useless. Some comments were talking about my lack of free content on social media, especially YouTube. I immediately noted it down, and started thinking of ways to plug that gap. They were absolutely right—if I was positioning myself as an expert and selling an information product, I needed to share a lot of content and value for free, so that people could try my products out for a limited period and decide to sign up. Lesson learnt. I worked on fixing that over the next few months.

Regarding the other, spineless hateful comments, I vowed to not let it affect me. In one of his podcasts, the famous American leadership expert John Maxwell had said, *"You need to keep your heart open, so it still hurts when it's supposed to."* The important thing to note here is you cannot close off your heart, stop looking at anything negative, and do things your own way. Because when something really needs to affect you, and change you for the better, your heart will be closed off.

The other hateful, mean, offensive stuff—you cannot look at it on a daily basis. I can be strong and act tough, but if the first thing I see on a daily basis are negative comments, I will never be productive. I will go into a spiral every single day. How on earth will I be able to run my company? On the heels of this incident, I hired a social media manager, and took their help to clean out any offensive emails and comments that I had no business seeing. I had so much peace of mind after this. I also focused on being so good at my job, in a way that my confidence came from within.

During that time, I focused on making my programs better so all my customers got results from it. Because results cannot be ignored, data cannot be denied. I decided to stop being emotional about business. Yes, we make money from our products. That's how businesses run. That's how I'm able to pay my team's salary and they are able to pay bills, that's how all our business expenses run, that's how I'm able to give to charity every month. But all of that is secondary to me.

I want our customers to get *real* life-changing results—not just feeling like *"Oh, this content was good"*—but really *"This content changed my life. It helped me quit my job and earn $5,000 a month or $10,000 a month in consistent income"*. That's what motivates me every single day, because while money is good, a lack of purpose, of pursuing something bigger than yourself, will lead to stagnation. Why are you doing this in the first place? You need to find something that keeps you going even if the world says mean things about you, even if your family is against it, even if the going gets tough. You need to find a why so strong that when life gets you down, you can anchor on that reason, to bring you back to your goals.

I learnt so many lessons from all of this. And I'm going to list them down for you, because I guarantee you, if you are on the path of doing something new, and you are putting it out in the world, you will meet the same hurdles. In hindsight, if I had expected this, it wouldn't have hurt so much and affected me so much. I would have learnt not to take it personally in the first place. But I didn't know. So, I'm hoping I can use this space to warn you, prepare you, and prepare your mindset so you don't let it kill your fire.

I love what John Green, the American author of many bestsellers including *The Fault in Our Stars,* said in one of his YouTube videos: *"Don't believe your hype, don't believe your haters"*. You shouldn't think about yourself as too cool, or put yourself on a pedestal ever. Walk on the ground, humble yourself. So that if a few people hate you, it doesn't affect your ego or self-esteem. Because after that phase, I promised myself: *I will never let anyone take away my fire, no matter what.*

I want you to know that…

Someone doing more than you, and someone who has achieved more than you will never ever have the time or energy to stop and type negative offensive comments on your content. It's always the people who are not working on their dreams, who have the time to shit on other people's dreams.

Take criticism and feedback. If you're getting similar kinds of feedback, stop and listen. What can I learn from this? What if I can use this feedback and be a better version of myself?

"They don't create statues of critics." I heard this quote somewhere and it has stayed with me. Always

remember this, they build statues of Mahatma Gandhi, and Nelson Mandela and Martin Luther King, and not of their assassins or the naysayers they faced.

Hire gatekeepers to protect your peace. Your peace of mind is too important to go through this nonsense on a daily basis. Hire a team, and train them to block/ban people as necessary. A pile of crap always attracts flies, so when someone starts a negative chain, more people will join in the fun. Hire your team to become your gatekeepers, so you can focus your time on doing your work which will help people.

Hurt people hurt people. When people write mean, offensive things, it says more about them than it does about you. Acknowledge that maybe this isn't about you. Perhaps they're hurting, or they have nothing going on in their life, or they were hurt by someone—so bless them, say a prayer for them, and wish them the best. When you don't care about them, it's freeing on another level.

Whenever you are trying to chase any dream, there will be so many people who will share their unsolicited opinions, negative comments, say something absolutely mean, and will crush your feelings. These could be close family members, relatives, friends, and even strangers on the internet. To quote my favourite singer, performer, and inspiration, Taylor Swift: "Shake it off."

Her journey of dealing with her naysayers really inspires

me. She dealt with shady behaviour from Kanye West when she was barely 19 years old. To being cancelled before her Reputation era, to her masters being sold without her permission, she has dealt with energy suckers and haters all her life. And yet, she still stands tall at the top of her game, 18 years into the game. If you had to choose, be a Taylor, not a Kanye!

So now you know about dealing with haters, and trolls. But I also want to tell you to have fun with trolls and haters. Because when you're running advertising for your business, more comments > more engagement > cheaper conversions. So, after I knew how to deal with it, I would pick some comments on my ads, and have fun with them. I'd answer in a sassy, sarcastic manner, which would make people laugh also while taking care to not offend the commenter. A fair warning: you need to grow thick skin before you do this.

Bye Bye, Comparison-itis

Imagine you are in a room full of 100 people. Now imagine, you're playing a weird game where you compare yourself to the appearances, money, fitness of these 100 people. Is this a comparison game you can win?

But we all do it every day, right. When we go on social media, and completely compare all aspects of our life to people showing their top 1 percent highlight reels. As someone who shares her content online and runs her entire business based on social media for the last nine years, I know I share a tiny fraction of my life online. I'm much happier when I'm off social media.

Recently, in coaching clients, I see a pattern arising. Where everyone is comparing. Which leads to self-esteem issues. And self-sabotage.

"Oh, she has so many more followers than me."
"Oh, he has so many friends and a better social life than me."
"Oh, she makes so much more money than me."
"Oh, he has a fitter body than me."

We spend hours each day, comparing our life to others. Instead of putting our head down, putting our blinkers on, and working on our own projects. There was a time when I used to open Instagram, first thing in the morning. Lying in bed, I used to scroll for almost an hour, before getting ready for the day. It was a vicious habit.

Mornings are sacred. I wasted precious energy that could have been spent doing "morning pages", a journaling practice that involves filling three sides of paper with words, stream of consciousness-style, first thing every day. Or I could have started my day with movement by doing yoga. Renowned computer scientist and public speaker, Dr. Cal Newport has said that social media is a product of the last decade, as a society we really don't know how to deal with it yet. So, we use it without any guidelines. For example, we know smoking is bad for our lungs. Or hard drugs are bad. But we don't view social media addiction as a vice as yet because it's still so new.

Creators with millions of subscribers go through depression and burnout because of this. They don't know what constitutes a healthy amount of time to spend on social media. Or that they should take social media detoxes often; to create boundaries with social media. As creators, we must delegate parts of our social media jobs to trusted team members so it doesn't deter the quality of our lives, and so that we can protect our mental health and self-esteem from unnecessary damage.

I like to create what I call 'white spaces' often. One week every quarter, I go for a complete social detox. It includes no social media apps, no communication apps, no news, no talking to anyone work-related at all. As creators and entrepreneurs, we need this white space to figure out what we want for ourselves, and not what the world wants us to do.

When I went to Bali last year for my birthday, I took nine days off social media completely. It was the happiest I had been in months. I went hiking. I went cycling. I explored Balinese villages with a local guide. I went rafting and swimming in the river. I took Batik painting classes held at a local's family home, where three generations lived together under one roof. I experienced local food and heard stories about life in Bali. I day dreamed of someday owning a rice field and a villa in Bali. I read books on my Kindle. I manifested and created intentions for my biggest dreams, some of which came true sooner than later.

I want all of us to love ourselves enough to not compare our life to a hundred strangers on social media. I want us to live our best lives off social media instead of constantly worrying about sharing real time stories, or do throwback posts immediately after coming back from our trips.

So Your Business Runs on Social Media. Here's What You Need to Know

I don't keep social media apps on my phone. Not even Slack or Gmail, which are important tools to run my company. No apps equal no losing impulse control. If I install those apps during big launches, I keep the notifications off so that these apps don't control me.

I download apps when I need to create content instead of mindlessly scrolling and consuming. I promptly delete it when the job is done.

I have worked on creating processes on quality control and delegated my social media management to my team. This way, I can spend time creating things, like writing and editing this book instead of mindlessly scrolling, getting down by looking at negative comments or getting sucked into the comparison game.

I have been creating an intentional white space every quarter, for a minimum of seven days. When I can afford to, I have two weeks of white space. My rule is to take seven days minimum off social media every 90 days. I call this the '7-90' detox rule. I invite you to try it out today.

Think about what you can do if you're not spending time online. Making being present a priority rather than being on social media. Listen to podcasts while working out instead of being on social media. Video call your parents or family or loved ones while taking a long walk through the park. Call your best friends and have long conversations with them instead of getting quick dopamine hits from social media. Watch a movie or a series instead of scrolling for hours. Read an actual book cover-to-cover instead of consuming social media. This is the best way to stand out and not have your content and brand look like anyone else's. On days when I'm unable to practice what I preach, I remind myself to trust myself to figure this out; give myself plenty of grace on days when I sometimes go past my intended screen time for the day.

If I ask you to check the screen time for your last week, what would it be? 50 hours? 30 hours? 10 hours? It's extremely important to disconnect from the online world and connect better with your inner world. We constantly get hit with jealousy and comparison on social media. Wouldn't it be nice to really connect with our own self? If you think you don't have enough time, check your screen time.

Trauma is a Tough Teacher

There was a time in my life a couple years ago when I cried straight up for a month because I was dealing with a trauma. Nothing I did helped me. I was still high-functioning from the outside. I showed up for work, led my team, took care of my clients, and did all the necessary things. But from the inside, I felt broken. It was a lot of things combined. We were recovering the COVID-19 pandemic—those two years saw so much heartbreak and loss and trauma.

I decided to go for a meditation retreat in Singapore. It was life-changing. We did multiple kinds of meditation. One of the practitioners taught us active meditation which was the best and most effective for me. It is about violently shaking and dancing with an eye mask on and it lasts for an hour—it's physically exhausting. And by the end I was in tears because it exudes all the energy being blocked in your body. I believe the body remembers a lot of our trauma and sadness and it needs to be let out.

Then there was a session about forgiveness. Where you wrote people's names on a piece of paper, and then put it in the fire, implying that they were ready to finally forgive them. That you were done holding grudges, that you were ready to free up space in your mind.

Then, I went through a full day of silence where we all didn't talk to anyone.

We all ate alone at our tables. We didn't even nod at each other, because even locking eyes and nodding is considered a form of communication. A full day of silence, not talking to people around you, not talking to loved ones back home but keeping the reception open for just your thoughts and feelings.

These practices have helped me a lot. I encourage you to find a meditation center near you and take their day classes, book a retreat in the mountains and give yourself some free space to heal from your traumas. I won't say that it healed me overnight. But progress was made. And isn't healing a journey and not a destination?

Life has kicked me in the belly several times. These were times I thought I'd never smile again, or travel again, or feel love again. Times when life was fucking hard or I wanted to burn my business to the ground or I felt so alone I thought I wanted to stop existing. But I always tell myself: *"Perhaps you had to go through it, so you can help others heal through it"*. Every human goes through varying degrees of trauma in life. It's not just people in warzones, or soldiers, or people dealing with calamities go through. If you had an experience that broke yourself from within, it's trauma.

And trauma can be the best teacher.
While you're going through it, you don't think of it as a teaching moment. You curse, you whine, you wallow in self-pity and think why me? I want to remind you that all of it is fair and allowed. However, if we don't heal through our trauma, it shows up in various forms: our body shows signs or it leads to mental health issues. So, let's not suppress it. Because the goal isn't to forget or heal overnight at all. It is to know that healing is a life-long journey and it's completely alright to take your own time. We are imperfect humans. In an imperfect universe.

What helps while dealing with trauma are simple foundational things:

1. Movement: Even moving for 30 minutes within your home, while listening to music counts. We need to remove the negative hormones from our body. We need to take the trash out. And movement, preferably outside in nature but even at home, helps release endorphins and makes you feel human again. Workout Habits are to be built in good times, so they lift us up in bad times.

2. Gratitude: It is fucking bad. But it could be worse. See what you can still find to be grateful for; a hug from a loved one, a chat with a friend, unexpected help coming to you, not having to worry about money, or having your health support you.

3. Self-leadership: While wallowing in self-pity feels good, and I recommend it to get it out of the system at the start. But then, knowing that sometimes our actions can have consequences, so seeing what we can learn from this experience. Or sometimes, life is just tough and the worst things happen to you through no fault of your own. In either case, know that YOU still hold the power to lead yourself out of it. By asking for help from a loved one, or a therapist or a professional.

4. Loved ones: Share, be vulnerable with your loved ones. And let them pour into you till you are able to take care of yourself.

5. Optimism: Nothing lasts forever. Nothing good. Nothing trauma related. And isn't that inspiring?

6. Flip the switch: Use the trauma, use the pain. If there is a date that is marred for you every year.

7. You can either be scared of it or dread it or go into a depressive state when it approaches.

8. Or this year, this time you can make it the best day ever. I used to dread a day every year, and would be a depressive mess when that day came through. It went on for a couple of years. But then I decided to take my family and had the best vacation of our lives. We have the power to decide what meaning a day or a situation has. We have the chance to flip

the switch. Every year going forward you'll look forward to that day as one of the happiest days of your life. We can choose to be in pain, blame others or the Universe for that shitty thing that happened to us—or we can take back control.

Sometimes bad things happen. Sometimes tough things happen accidentally. But that doesn't impact the long run. It only impacts the future if you let it. The meaning you assign to and the importance you give to it matters. You're giving a bigger real estate in your brain than it deserves. We cannot fix the world or make it better while still dealing with our heavy weight experiences. We need to heal, we need to let it go.

I will leave you with this lovely poem by the Scottish writer Donna Ashworth:

You don't move on after loss, but you must move with. You must shake hands with grief, welcome her in, for she lives with you now. Pull her a chair at the table and offer her comfort. She is not the monster you first thought her to be. She is love. And she will walk with you now, stay with you now, peacefully. If you let her. And on the days when your anger is high, remember why she came, remember who she represents. Remember. Grief came to you, my friend, because love came first.
Love came first.

Homework: Journal It Out

I know this may seem too woo-woo or too spiritual, but please trust me on this and journal with me. When the hopelessness hits, here's what I ask myself:

"If the Universe made you a promise, to give you all your deepest desires and dreams. With no conditions. No transaction. No shame. Asking for nothing and no-one in return. What will you ask of the Universe?"

Write down the top things that pop up here. You know it, your heart knows it. You don't need me or anyone else to tell you this. In your deepest heartfelt desires, you already know.

Trust that knowing. Don't judge that knowing. Don't shame yourself for having those desires. You are not less worthy or greedy or small or weak because of those desires. They just are, accept them.

I hope you have written these dreams down before proceeding.

"Now, how will the person who has achieved all their dreams show up? How will they execute, what do they say, how do they carry themselves?"

Write it down. What kind of clothes do they wear, where do they live, who are the people they hang out with, what kind of content do they consume, what kind of books they read, what kind of accountability do they show, how do they behave in adversity, how do they treat the people around them.

"Now, we all know the Universe is powerful but it doesn't just give things to us. What will it take for you to believe that you are the chosen one that deserves and is meant for all these desires. What will it take?"

Do I need someone to give me a contract and tell me that these desires will come true 100 percent and I just have to sign this contract? Do I need someone to come and show me the future?

Or…

Do I need someone to tell me if it will never come true and it's all preposterous and impossible? And will I give this person too much power to actually believe in this mindset. In this case, I would rebel and tell that person to fuck off and that they know nothing. And then I would work extra hard to prove them wrong.

And so, logically in both scenarios, so there's no guarantee in life. There's no guarantee that you'll succeed or that you'll fail. You'll just have to roll the dice and cross that bridge to find out.

Here's also what I tell myself often:

I have to believe it will happen.
I have to believe that it is happening right now.
It's just not reached me fully, it's on its way.
If it happens great, if it doesn't happen also great.
Because something much better is on their way.
This or something better!

Chapter 15

How To Face Your Fears

Writing this book was becoming a hard, hard journey for me. I thought it was supposed to be hard and painful.

I hated typing so much while also dealing with my usual day to day work where I already have to type so much and then also having to, you know, write a book along the way. Running a business full-time which needed my attention and finding time to complete the book was challenging for me.

So, I decided to start creating voice notes and recording it into a software which would then transcribe the text in real time, which has been incredibly helpful. And then I would just put this text into a software like Grammarly, which would help me fix the grammar and words and make the text presentable to distill my ideas and my thoughts. I don't have to type so much while already suffering from back pain because of sitting for long hours on the laptop.

I came across a book by Chris Fox titled *5,000 Words Per Hour: Write Faster, Write Smarter.* It's an incredible book, very succinct, to the point, and gives you many tips about increasing your writing speed. Among them, the author mentions that you can speak faster than you can write. There, I found an easier solution to get the first draft written faster! So, I started to write about 1,000 words within five minutes of speaking, which is crazy. That is how I intend to complete the remaining 20,000 words of my pending first draft.

Believe it or not, the first draft has been a work in progress since the last three years. I wrote the first 18,000 words in October 2020. Then somehow life and my business took over and I wasn't able to work on it. Nearly three years later, in May 2023, I worked on the rest and wrote 35,000 words—and have kind of been stuck since. But you're reading this book now, so obviously the first draft has been done. And so have multiple drafts after to get the book out to you.

There's always a simpler way. You could also hire a ghostwriter if that makes the process easy for you. And things don't need to be torturous; things can get done in an easier way. You just have to find it and you just have to believe it. Tell me, what is the one big dream you're stuck on right now? Write down 10 creative ideas to get it done. And make it easy on yourself. Do it now.

The intention of the first draft is just to exist, and then it can get better.

*

If you have been liking the book, I would really appreciate it if you would share it on your social media and share how the book impacted you the most. If you have a friend or a family's birthday coming up and you feel like they need this message of making wealthy moves, please share the book with them. I would really appreciate it, because it truly has been a labour of love.

I'm not doing this for money.

But I hope the message of wealthy moves goes to every woman and man out there who needs it, who wants to grab it, who wants to implement it, who wants to use it. To enhance their lives. Because that would make me the happiest girl in the whole world.

This book took its own time. I was struggling to write this book while also running my business full time, dealing with fires, and taking care of my clients. So, it was difficult for me to prioritize writing. I was kind of ignoring the promises I made to myself that I would write something every single day.

Last April, I went to Bali to write, and it turned out to be a great writing trip. I had written around 5,300 words at that time. However, everything got set aside due to day-to-day life, social events, and business matters. A few weeks ago, *I decided that writing the book is going to be easy,* not tough or overwhelming.

My brain worked to find a better solution. I stopped sleeping with my phone at night to avoid getting distracted in the morning. Instead, I started my day by reading a couple of chapters from my book to ground myself in a positive way. While reading, I found ideas bubbling up in my head about what I wanted to say in the book. Writers are great readers, and sometimes what you read sparks your own ideas and stories. It reminds you of forgotten childhood stories or emotional times, which you now want to share.

So now, every morning, I use a tool called Otter.ai. I dictate and speak into my iPad, avoiding the overwhelming task of starting with a blank piece of paper. Otter.ai captures the audio and transcribes it to text in real time. This practice lets me write 800 to 1,000 words each day in about 30 minutes. I'm aware that I will need to edit it later, but at least the first draft is done. The first draft only needs to exist; it doesn't need to be perfect or ready for publishing.

I read a blog article from Tim Ferriss on his website about public speaking depths. He introduced the EPE framework—it stands for Example, Point, Example.

This framework has been life-changing for me.

When I need to create a YouTube video, I use this format. I have three main points, and for each, I provide an example. The EPE framework forces me to think about examples and stories while writing. This makes content more engaging and memorable. Using frameworks like this doesn't mean starting from scratch. Apply constraints and patterns to your creative work. If you're writing a book chapter, use a three-point framework. For YouTube videos, speeches, Video Sales Letters, or webinars, use the EPE framework.

Creativity benefits from constraints; they make you more engaging and execution-focused. For example, when I first started writing this book, I had no outline, no chapter flow and I let myself run wild. The consequence was that it was haphazard and I was writing about anything and everything without a proper narrative structure. Then I decided to put constraints and actually create an outline, which made my life simpler.

I think for doing anything worthwhile you should be able to embrace fear. But only if it was easy. In this chapter, I'm going to show you a few steps to stop being scared and start chasing fear.

I do this process of journaling before any big goal I want to achieve. I've learned how to analyze fears and how to get over them. And how to not let your fears cripple you to take no action. I had so many fears about writing this book and I still do while I'm writing them.

Things like…

What if I fail, publicly, after I've already announced to my audience of 300,000 that I'm writing a book? What if I'm unable to finish it or what if I do publish it, and people hate it?

What if I'm vulnerable in the book because I want to help people, but I also don't want to be humiliated by sharing my failures and fears?

What if publishing this book negatively affects my business in some way or the other?

What if I publish this book and no one buys it, and I would have publicly failed?

At the same time, I was fearful about succeeding as well. What if I actually become successful and have a multi-million-dollar business that impacts one million people?

If somehow my business makes more money than ever, maybe more than my husband, will it end our relationship? Will I end up lonely? Being successful would mean I have to sacrifice my family, my work life balance, and always be hustling.

Success in business would mean more people I can help

but also an increase in trolls, haters. Success in business will somehow hamper my safety because sometimes people are just horrible.

What has worked for me, is journaling it all down, because it allows me to analyze each of my fears and break them down in detail.

"What if I fail, publicly, after I've already announced to my audience of 300,000 that I'm writing a book? What if I'm unable to finish it or what if I publish it, and people hate it?"

Failure is feedback. If people buy the book, and hate it, then I would have more feedback than ever to work on for my next book. If I never write the book, I would have zero feedback, and a huge regret in my heart. Do I want to have this regret in my heart when I'm 80 that I never even wrote and published the book just because of fear of failure? In fact, I'm not hoping this book will be a bestseller at all, I just want to get the first one out of the way, so I can get incredible feedback to work on more books which would have more potential to be a bestseller.

What if I'm vulnerable in the book because I want to help people, but I also don't want to be humiliated by sharing my failures and fears?

If my being vulnerable can help even 10 people, be more courageous with their dreams, or suck up and start working towards their dreams, then it would be worth it. And every successful person I know has failed, because that's the only way to succeed. So there's no shame in failing. In fact, there's more shame in never having tried, because that's a choice you made.

"What if publishing this book negatively affects my business in some way or the other?"

I don't know if this book will do more harm or be better for my business. The goal is to help as many people as possible with my story and experience of building a million-dollar business and to inspire people to own their dreams and craft their dream life. But what if people stop buying my products, because this book is good that it helps them…that is a good problem to have, haha. On the flip side, what if this book is so bad, that it tarnishes my brand I've worked so hard to create for eight years, and people stop buying my products.

But here's the thing. If I won't write it, won't publish it, I will never know. I solemnly believe this book can help anyone reading it, so if I won't publish it, I'm doing a disservice to all the people I can help—but also doing a disservice to my hopes and dreams.

"What if I publish this book and no one buys it, and I would have publicly failed?"

This one is a doozy. All I tell myself is this: I already have over 4,000 customers at the time of writing this.

If they bought a pricier product, they would be willing to buy this book too. And if this book can help even a 1,000 people, that's going to be worth it. That's why I keep going for now. If people make fun of me for publicly failing, I know it won't be those people who have achieved more than me, because they don't have time to do it and know what it takes to succeed in the book writing process. It's only people who do less than me that might make fun of me, and I don't care about them.

If I give up now, I will never ever write anything good. So, I have to keep going, and get this book out of the way, so I can write better and more books.

"If somehow my business makes more money than ever, maybe more than my husband, will it end our relationship? Will I end up lonely?"

I believe you can have everything in the world that you wish for. Just not at the same time. If I work actively towards my relationships and family, without sacrificing them, or being a workaholic, or by sacrificing my mental and physical health, then this can be done. Did someone write in the sky that "successful women entrepreneurs cannot have successful relationships too?" No.

So you see, I journal it out. Sometimes it takes me more than one pass at journaling to get some perspective on things. You need to reason out your excuses and self-limiting beliefs and actually question your feelings and separate them from the facts. I know you have deep felt desires and dreams. Maybe it's writing a book, maybe it's pursuing your PhD degree abroad at age 40, or maybe it's being a full-time world traveller. Whatever it is, I know you can chase your fears and I know you can get everything that you desire.

Homework: Journal It Out

What is the big project that is in your heart but you feel stuck on?

What worries, thoughts, fears are popping in your mind when you think about executing the BIG project?

Journal where each worry is deriving from, the root of it, and walk yourself through a better perspective that supports you in taking action.

Chapter 16

Tiny Habits and Healthy Moves

My dad taught me to swim when I was three years old. Back then, my parents would bribe me with amazing snacks to motivate me to learn swimming, and it worked because all I wanted was the opportunity to devour those snacks and be a happy kid. Did your parents encourage you to learn a sport in your childhood? Because it is only now that I have come to appreciate the importance of developing skills that bring the mind and body together in amazing ways.

Now, as an adult juggling education, job, career, family, and personal life, managing your mental health and battling traumas while being high-functioning, we forget that the things taught to us in our childhood were actually for our own benefit. So, I recommend digging deep and rediscovering the sport you used to enjoy as a kid. Health really is wealth! It could be swimming, basketball, cricket, baseball, soccer, table tennis, badminton, or anything else. Take it up again, and join a class nearby your community to have other friends to play with. Engaging in sports is great for your body, mind, and making new friends, especially if you've moved to a new city or country.

I take my workout routine seriously, not because I'm vain and want to look great in the mirror (although that's one small reason), but because life taught me the hard way when I was diagnosed with Polycystic Ovary Syndrome (PCOS). This led to significant weight gain, facial cystic acne, and a huge dent in my self-confidence. And every time you meet people who start suggesting their best acne antidote, without being asked, gets annoying really fast.

I decided to take my health seriously and hired a nutritionist for six months to help me figure it out, improve my eating habits, and started enjoying workouts. My workout routine includes a 25-kilometer bike ride in a nearby park by the beach, swimming in the pool at my condominium complex, going to the gym for a 12:4:30 session (a great workout that burns around 250 calories by setting the treadmill at 12 incline, 4 mph speed for 30 minutes), and doing some bicep curls and upper body exercises to improve my posture and neck problems. Some days, I go for a walk while talking to my friends who are spread out all over the world or chat with my parents every single day while I'm walking to the park. Sometimes, I join a yoga session where the instructor pushes me hard, but in the end, I feel stronger and more grounded.

My main advice to you is not to treat exercise as work, but to learn how to enjoy it.

When you enjoy it, it will not feel like a chore. I like to put on a podcast from one of my favorite podcasters or play my favourite music while working out in the gym or cycling around. You can also choose to play this audiobook while working out the next time! I'm being cheeky, I know!

Daily movement is a key for me to maintain my mental health, ensure that my body is mostly disease-free, and keep it strong enough to combat anything that comes my way. Up until three years ago, I was treating my body like a garbage can—putting anything and everything in, without ever stopping for a moment to think about what I was doing. I was always stressed out, overweight and didn't feel great all the time. I slept after midnight and complained about not having 100 percent energy the next day. All my unhealthy eating habits and being overweight led to dealing with face acne, which again gave way to body image issues. I hated my face, my body and didn't want to show up on camera barefaced; sometimes, I mustered some courage to show up on camera but only after applying a bag of makeup.

I barely had any good habits to hold me over when bad times hit. So anytime I faced a setback or a failure, I used to go into a depression and anxiety spiral. I wouldn't "feel" like doing anything, or was unable to get out of bed for days, and would keep crying on end. I also was a bit short-tempered, reckless, and not much of a people person. I certainly wouldn't have been able to handle the challenges that come with serving thousands of customers and leading a team well—if I hadn't gotten my shit together.

I don't recognize that person anymore. That doesn't mean I'm a monk now, and eat clean all the time and never lose my mind. I'm not perfect, no one is. But I was able to minimize all my unhealthy ways and maximize my productive ways to deal with things happening around me. And that's where habits come in.

Here's the thing, building a business is nothing less than a roller coaster ride. Some days are great where you feel like you're on top of the world, some other days you feel like a dumpster fire and hope to hide yourself away from everyone. This also means that the anxiety kicks in not just about the huge things like revenue, customer results, but also small things like "Do I deserve weekends off"? I had major anxiety leading up to the weekend, because for my business to survive and grow, I thought I needed to be working 24/7. I succumbed to the hustle culture. My anxiety kept giving me all kinds of negative thoughts about how if I took time off for my own sanity, bad things would happen. Bad things like people commenting hateful stuff on social media, or customers asking their money back or our revenue tanking because I wasn't working hard. I'm not kidding, it could get pretty debilitating.

I have had to coach myself through even basic things like taking time off during weekends is completely alright. In fact, it means I'm more productive during the week to deal with any business challenges. I also Googled if anyone else was facing the same worries, watched through videos of the trailblazers and thought leaders before me. That really helped. But the most important thing that helped with my anxiety was a bunch of good habits.

1. Meditation
2. Being grateful everyday
3. Journalling
4. Eating clean
5. Working out
6. Hydration
7. Sleeping right

Now, after reading this list you might think this is the most basic thing on Earth! You're right, they're basic. But most of the time, we try to solve things in the most complicated manner when really our basics are out of whack. Fix your basics first, then try other fancy things.

These habits have changed my life and helped me to get be healthier; my skin glows, I have more energy which means I am able to work better and harder; I feel like I'm taking care of my mind and body, which feels awesome instead of treating them like rubbish; I can handle anxiety whenever it creeps in, because anxiety will always accompany desire, and hope and determination. It's what makes us human.

The benefits of the following habits are endless, so let me talk about each of them in detail.

Meditation

There was a time in my life when I meditated every single day first thing when I woke up. I started with just meditating for three minutes a day and then gradually increased it. I can now meditate for 15 minutes without getting distracted. Start small, you can do anything for three minutes. I like to meditate while listening to soothing spiritual songs from YouTube, or sometimes I like to use a meditation app called Headspace. I highly believe my temper and anxiety-management improved so much in the last couple of years because of this habit.

Meditation calms, relaxes and grounds me. I'm not asking you to learn some fancy kind of meditation or anything. I'm asking you to sit straight for 10 minutes without looking at your phone or being distracted, focus on your breathwork, and let your thoughts flow. Meditation isn't about having zero thoughts, but it's about letting your thoughts pass through your mind without reacting to them.

Here's something else about anger and anxiety, especially which comes through by reacting to what other people are saying about you or what other people are doing to you. If you always react to other people, they rule you, your peace and your sanity. For our own happiness and sanity, it's important to not react immediately or ever depending on the circumstances. Meditation has helped so much in that. I can only control my own behaviour, my own thoughts and actions. What others do to me is their own problem, not mine. It's helped so much to realize that I am in control and I won't be shaken from my core and calmness so damn easily. It's incredibly freeing when you master the ability to not let other people shake you and suck you into their drama and conflict. Meditation is a wealthy person's secret weapon!

Habit Criteria: *"I meditate for 15 minutes at 7 am every day in my office."*

Being Grateful Everyday

I start my day by jotting down five things I'm grateful for in my journal every single day. Jot down not just generic things like "grateful for my home" but to go deep and be grateful for moments in the last 24 hours; specifically, like "grateful for that deep conversation I had Thursday night with my husband", or "grateful for soothing hot coffee during winters", or "grateful for my team member Fazia because she stepped up and handled business challenges", or "grateful for conversations with my mom and how loving she is". Details matter.

When you do this, you will be on the lookout for such small beautiful moments during the day, and will be able to start the next morning right by reminiscing about them. Admittedly, being grateful has cut down on how much I would whine and complain. When we're grateful, we realize we already have got so much to cherish in our lives.

The thing about social media is that we love watching other people's stories and keeping up with their travels but it leads to a lot of jealousy and comparison. We compare our lives to their highlights and then feel bad about our own life. We see other people making more money, or flying in a jet plane, or buying luxury clothes while you are stuck, either trying to keep things up at home, or slogging at work.

But, when we think about everything we're grateful for, we learn to be content in what we have right now. And to stop comparing other people's highlights to our own down phases.

Habit Criteria: *"I write five things in my gratitude journal every morning at 7:15 am while sitting on my purple sofa in my office."*

Journalling

I tend to do freestyle journaling on a need basis. When I

feel anxious or stressed or unhappy, I pop out my journal to process what I'm going through. I write my heart out without stopping myself. I write as if no one is going to read it ever. I don't judge myself for feeling this way or writing it down—I just let it flow. At the end of this vent session, I will feel lighter. Since everything is out on paper, I'm able to analyze the core reasons behind why I'm stressed or anxious. Most times, I will also make a list of things I can do to get myself out of this situation or not feel like it in the first place in the future.

Journaling is therapeutic for me. Sometimes I will also make a video if I'm too lazy to write and will coach myself through what I'm feeling and the reasons behind it. The main thing is to process your worries in a format that works best for you. For some, it may be journalling, for others it may be talking to a friend or a loved one, for some it may be recording videos and processing their worries through it. Do it anyway because I promise you that bottling up your worries and stress isn't going to make anything better. In fact, it affects your productivity and also your relationships with other people.

Habit Criteria: *"Whenever I'm feeling stressed or anxious, I write my heart out in a journal and process it. If I don't possess a journal, I will record a video wherever I am."*

Eating Clean

For me, food is joy. I absolutely love eating a variety

of things. It makes me so happy. I'm one of those "live to eat" kind of people. Growing up, I didn't have the freedom to eat out a lot. So, I would crave chocolates and chips every week, and sometimes, Mom would let me buy these things, but other times it was a strict no. Which made me very upset.

When I became the master of my own life, I did everything that baby Roota wasn't allowed to do. Baked goods were my best friends. Going out and eating cheesy yummy continental food was my hobby. In my travels, I would not watch what I ate and indulged in everything from scrumptious Parisian pastries to pastas in Rome to noodles in Indonesia. My mouth is already watering so I'll stop. But you get the gist.

Suffice to say, years of living like this didn't bode well with my health. So, when I was diagnosed with PCOS, I had to get my shit together. It's been a long journey to improve my relationship with food, and I'm not fully there yet, but I'm sharing a few things that I've learnt along the way.

I no longer eat food because it will go to waste, or it will go bad. If I don't feel like eating it or crave it, I will not eat it for the sake of eating it. I would rather call someone and donate the food. I eat intentionally. I won't order unhealthy stuff because I don't feel like making myself lunch. I try to find healthier options like a salad instead of ordering in tacos. I eat tasty stuff only when I crave it. Not because someone around me is eating it because they're craving it or because it's already there at home. I have started becoming very aware of what exactly I'm craving, and only then indulging in it.

I've learnt how to cook and make things which are healthy and yummy. In most cases, that usually happens when you cook at home or have someone cook for you. There are so many YouTube channels which cover recipes according to your taste buds and culture. At some point, I was obsessed with trying the new superfoods like quinoa or broccoli. I used to think that the food I ate as a child wasn't healthy enough. But that's grossly incorrect. After working with a nutritionist, I've learned that the food our grandparents ate is balanced and our body is already used to it.

I don't diet, ever. Even when my mom used to make me fast during some days of the year, it was torture for me. I don't do intermittent fasting or Keto or Paleo or whatever is in these days. I do what is scalable, what I can do every single day for the rest of my life. While one of these trendy fad diets might get you results in the short term, they cannot be implemented forever and you will gain back more weight than before.

I don't focus on the number on the scale or how I look. Although I must say glowing skin is a great bonus! I want to eat clean and healthy because I want to feel great. I don't want to feel sluggish and have less energy. I want to feel awesome and agile. Like an athlete! That's also one of my affirmations: "I am an athlete!"

Eating with awareness—my nutritionist advised me to not eat strictly in front of the TV or while watching Netflix, or while listening to music, or while reading. Now, when I eat, I try to focus completely on my food. I savour and enjoy every single bite of my food. The taste, smell and sound—all senses are triggered which keeps you full longer, you don't need to eat as much, plus when I eat with awareness, I crave things less because I was able to enjoy it so well the last time.

Habit Criteria: *"I'm allowed to eat everything. I eat my favourite foods and what I crave, I eat in limited portion sizes. I choose healthy foods 90 per cent of the time because I'm grateful that my body supports me."*

Workouts

I intend to move my body for 30 minutes every single day. Please note, there are days and weeks when I am unable to move everyday but the intention is there. I'm not perfect and this is still a journey for me. The best mindset shift I did to workout more regularly was that instead of doing something I hated, I tried a bunch of things that I actually liked doing.

For example, I hate going to the gym, I get uneasy from being around people who are fitter, and I hate when the machines I want to use are completely hogged by other people. I also feel a thousand times more comfortable working out on my own so I can wear what I want and admire my ab babies coming through. So, I stopped forcing myself to go to the gym and instead tried a bunch of home workouts.

I realized I loved dancing, so I love to start my workouts by dancing to my favourite songs. Beyonce's music gives me a great start and I'm in the mood then. Then, I do resistance training by following a fitness app and target upper body, lower body and full body on different days of the week. I follow an app because I totally need guidance with warmups, cooldowns, reps and forms of each exercise. I don't want to keep wondering if what I'm doing is the right form or is a substantial workout that is making a difference. So, I blindly follow the app.

I invest in the right tools and then follow the experts in everything—life and business! If you can hire a personal trainer and love working with someone for accountability, do that. If you love going to the gym, go do that. If you are a yoga person, be that person. If you love weight-training, be ripped, my friend. I also love wearing cute gym clothes which make me feel awesome while working out. Baggy sweatpants and loose tee shirts will make me feel more larger than I am but if I'm wearing flattering clothes, I am more motivated to look and feel good.

What I do know is what works for others, doesn't work for me. And what works for me, might not work for you. So try a bunch of things and create a workout routine for you. Define the time, location and type of workout and schedule that thing in your calendar. Your turn now.

Stop reading right now, and schedule your workouts for the month right now.

Habit criteria: *"I workout at 6 pm in my office. I do the Lower body workout from the Sweat app today."*

Hydration

If you ever get a chance to talk to Rachit, my partner, he will promptly say that this is my most annoying habit. I drink a lot of water, which means road trips with me are an absolute nightmare. I need to stop every couple hours, and relieve myself which annoys him to no end.

I'm sorry, but hydration is no joke. Drinking water is the most important thing for your body to function and remove the toxins. I'm not going to go deep into science here but know that so many diseases can be avoided by just drinking your damn water. I know of a few people who don't even drink one litre of water a day, and I'm absolutely shocked.

Guys, you need at least three litres of water intake daily. Use an app to track your water intake and set reminders to drink water if you're bad at remembering it. Personally, I like to aim for four litres a day and it keeps me hydrated and happy.

I always fill up my water bottles in the morning, and keep them on my work desk so there's no excuse to skip it. Whenever I'm doing coaching calls, I will always have a bottle with a straw so I can drink water peacefully while not making that gulping sound in front of hundreds of people.

Make things work for you, instead of making excuses for your hydration. If you take one thing from this book, please let it be this one. Drink your water, dammit!

Sleeping Right

Sleep is the *most* important thing. More important than diet, working out or even water. Yes, alright, I know above I said water is the most important thing, but really sleep trumps it. Hydration may be my favourite thing ever though, no one can debate that.

But seriously though, you need eight hours of sleep, period. I don't believe or relate to people who say you just need five-six hours, etc. Maybe you are the loin-child of Lord Zeus and have infinite energy with just five hours of sleep but I am merely an ordinary human. And I freaking need my eight hours.

Currently, I have my sleep schedule right on track. I sleep at 10:40 pm and get up at 6:40 am. This timing works perfectly right now but even though I might slightly move the timings around as per seasons, I still manage to sleep between 10-11:30 pm and will wake up from 6-8 am. Waking up before 7 am makes me feel super productive, I leap out of bed and jump right into my morning routine.

It's not simply how long you sleep that will make you feel good in the morning, but how well you rest your body. There are a few things I swear by to ensure good quality sleep.

1. Keep the room cool, you can't sleep when you feel hot. I also keep a cozy soft blanket with me to regulate the hotness/coolness of my body without getting up to do major fan/AC changes.

2. Two hours before bedtime, I get off social media. I try to stop watching TV an hour before I sleep, and I eat the last meal of the day three-four hours before I sleep.

3. Taking a bath before sleeping does wonders for you.

4. I drink chamomile tea because it will make your body wind down to sleep on time.

5. Yellow lights, not bright white lights, are your friend prior to sleeping.

6. If you've moved your body during the day, getting tired and sleeping will not be a problem.

Habit Criteria

Let's talk about Habit criteria. Good habits carry you through your bad days. Habit criteria are specific statements I create for myself, and add them to my to-do list daily or weekly, depending on the frequency I need to do them. I also like to be hyper-specific when I create these habit criteria. For example, I will note down: *"I workout at 6 pm in my office. I do the lower body workout from the Sweat app today."* Make sure you are as specific as possible with the time and place when you're jotting down these habit criteria.

For me, this level of clarity helps my brain already visualize doing that activity at a specific time; and there's no confusion about how the habit should be executed. Every aspect of it has been addressed in the note. It makes things easy for you and you avoid decision fatigue when the time comes to actually execute these habits. Save yourself the trouble of backing away from performing the habit itself.

If there's one book I recommend to every single person I meet, it is *Atomic Habits; An Easy & Proven Way to Build Good Habits & Break Bad Ones* by James Clear. I love that book and wish I could quote so many passages from it, but you should go pick up a copy and read it cover-to-cover.

However, big or small your dreams may be, you need relentless focus to make them come true. That means, not being distracted by social media, partying, wasting time or binge-watching Netflix every single day. Social media is amazing and I've built my entire million-dollar business on it—but it's also killing people's dreams.

Social media, scrolling and likes, give you instant gratification leading to a quick dopamine release. You might feel like not focusing on your bigger important tasks but feel like scrolling through the social apps all day long. Make sure to take social media detox breaks if your screen time is reaching an unhealthy level. If you're scrolling Instagram or TikTok for three hours daily, that's 90 hours every month and 1,080 hours during the year.

That is time you could have spent working on your next big novel or your next product. Your time and energy is limited, so use it wisely. Be drastic if you need to. Delete social media apps during the weekends and vacations; maybe even use two phones—one for social media posting and running your business, and the other one without any apps. Pick up the first phone for posting content rather than mindlessly consuming it. Do what you promise you will do without fail. If you've decided to wake up at 7 am, do it. If you've decided to go for a bike ride on Sunday, do it. If you've decided to take up yoga classes, follow through.

This might seem like a small thing but actions like these compound and work wonders for your mental health and sanity. You don't need to post every single meal you had or every place you visited—you can actually enjoy the present, actually pay attention to the conversations, smiles and bond with the people you're meeting with, or keep starting at the sea while a host of yachts, boats and water skiers pass you by. Enjoy the simple things, without any need to document everything.

Homework: Journal It Out!

Which habit criteria will you start implementing today onwards?

What lies have you told yourself about your healthy moves that are no longer serving you?

Which workout or activity can you enjoy for 30 minutes a day without it feeling like a drag?

Chapter 17

Your Wealthy Moves

My mentors have helped me so much to become the person I am today. I always believe in investing money to achieve faster growth strategically. You only have limited time available on Earth. Smart people know when to invest money and trade it for time. When you invest in a mentor, you're able to tap into years of their experience, failures, wisdom and know-how. You're investing money to save more of your time.

I'm not asking you to spend money you don't have for mentors. You should always spend money you have rather than taking loans. But people sometimes are so motivated to save a tiny amount of money and are willing to go through more frustration and stay overwhelmed rather than investing in getting help.

I want you to know that the most successful people have mentors and all the help in the world. Any of the greats you admire has or had a coach—Roger Federer, Michael Jordan, Serena Williams, Bill Gates—everyone! You don't need to invest millions of dollars to get help and mentorship from someone. You only need to find someone who is 10 steps ahead of you, and figure out how to learn from them by investing in their services and products.

In fact, when I was starting out as a freelancer, I had very little savings in my bank account. I didn't want to waste my money by investing in anything or anyone. I was trying to figure out freelancing, getting clients and growing my business all by myself. I was able to get a couple of clients without any help from a mentor; it was all good until it wasn't. Because running a business isn't as easy as just getting a customer. You want to ensure the customer is satisfied and happy with your product or service.

I didn't know how to keep my clients happy or how to get them results, which meant I was doing something wrong because I saw other people being very successful at freelancing. I was missing something that they knew.

I realized it was time. Time to invest in knowledge because I was tired of spinning my wheels around. I didn't want to give up in business, I had barely started. I didn't want to go back to a job working for a boss and building other people's dreams. I invested in my first course, and it changed everything for me. I learnt so much about marketing and getting clients, and skills I use to date. I became a champion of investing in mentors and courses after that.

If you want to learn to play guitar, go ahead and learn it from watching YouTube videos. But YouTube videos cannot tell you what exactly you're doing wrong if you're unable to hit a note right or play a song. If you invest in a personal guitar coach, they will tell you minute things which make a huge difference: like holding your finger in just a different place makes you sound better, or why you're unable to hit a particular note. It's that 1 percent guidance that makes you win.

Michael Phelps is an American swimmer who holds the record for the most Olympics medals won by any athlete at 28—including 23 gold medals and 13 individual golds. In 2008, he finished one-hundredth of a second ahead of his competitor, Milorad Cavic from Serbia. Phelps won the gold by that slimmest of margins! *1/100th of a second.* That's how small a difference it takes to win.

And that's why you need a mentor to help you grow.

If I invest in a $1,000 product which is going to help me do things better, it is going to help me make 10 times more money in the long term. This is why I have invested close to $100,000 already in my growth and learning in the past nine years.

How to Find Mentors

It is unreasonable to expect your mentors to teach you for free. Mentors are typically successful in their field, which means they are incredibly short on time and value their time well. Don't ask anyone to mentor you for free, unless you have something they want in return.

Make a list of five or 10 people who are doing exactly what you want to be doing in your life and business; remember they go hand in hand. Devour all of their content, books, free resources and learn from them. Pay attention to their style of teaching, their story, their failures and how customer obsessed they are. Checkout what premium training or products they have that can help you achieve your goals faster. Free content will only take you so far, the fastest way to get results is to invest in structured premium courses, coaching, conferences and masterminds.

Keep investing in your growth to ascend levels in business. The more access level you can get to your mentor, the faster will be your growth. But the more the personal access, the more investment it will be, so it's perfectly alright to invest in the mentor's services and products which meet your current goals and the financial investment you are comfortable with. You don't need to pay $100,000 for a one-day meetup with your mentor when you can buy their $1,000 course to learn the skills they can teach you.

Three Decisions That Matter

"There are 3 decisions that are the most important decisions you will make in your life: Who you marry, Where you live, What work you do."
Naval Ravikant, The Almanack of Naval Ravikant

What Work You Do

We spend the majority of our time working. Typically, that's eight-twelve hours out of 24 hours; so we spend at least one-third of our lives working. And another good chunk thinking about work, and letting our happiness or unhappiness be defined by our work. We spend a lot of time with our work peers. Make sure they're good people you like.

Work creates fulfillment. Stop wasting time finding passion. Do the most meaningful thing that makes sense now. For me, I did my software development job, then my travel blog, then freelancing, then my online education company, then writing books and creating videos. I didn't sit and wonder about my passion. You just have to take action.

Action gives you clues about what you need to do. Action is the only way to beat overwhelm. Action is the only way to beat under-confidence. Action is the only way to beat imposter syndrome.

Choosing what you get to do with your time is the

wealthiest move. Choose well.

Who You Marry

In my early 20s, I thought long and hard about whether I wanted to get married. I'd seen too many marriages in Indian culture and I didn't see what I liked. I thought to myself if I can change the parts I don't like, then having a life-long partner who I genuinely like, not just love, that would be cool. It would be like being assigned a best friend to do life with forever.

It is the most important decision of your life. I've seen people around me marry really bad people and it has effectively led to a lot of heartache. Or jumped into a relationship too quickly, got married and didn't end well. If you're in a bad relationship, you possess the power to get the hell out of it. If you're not in one, you have the power to choose the best one for yourself.

I also avoid sharing too many details, pictures and videos of my family on social media, because I believe people who share everything about their relationship online have something to prove to the world. Relationships, especially a marriage, are a lot of freaking hard work. So, don't believe the hype that PDA-sharing couples create online. It's two imperfect humans trying to survive and thrive. Sometimes, the growth of these two people tends to be tangential, rather than parallel, which also seems like the reason for a lot of divorces we see today.

If you find your love too early in life, then you have not become your own individual adult yet. And a lot of growth comes from learning to be happy solo, and together. I have adapted the mindset of joyfully present together rather than happily ever after. Relationships and marriage need a lot of work, and choosing the right partner for yourself is one of the best wealthy moves you can make.

Where You Live

I was really unhappy in the city I lived in for most of my adult life. I hated pollution and lack of safety and the lack of nature where I lived for seven years.

I moved out and had the best four years in Singapore. The rainy weather, the greenery and the lifestyle in Singapore was a massive upgrade. My current home base is Dubai. I get to live in one of the safest countries in the world, filled with incredible opportunities and beaches.

You can manifest where you live. You can choose a new adventure, a new country, a new city for your life. You have just one life. Stop adjusting and composing on your dreams. Stop saying, maybe someday. Stop making excuses that you can't move because of family, job or whatever. Everything can be figured out. If you have the intention that is. And if you lead yourself through it.

Meet Duality

In your journey of making wealthy moves, I think duality is a beautiful concept to be aware of.

Perfection is a myth, meet duality.
Duality is beautiful.
You can be caught up in your traumas, and still belly laugh when a loved one cracks a hilarious joke.

Pain and joy can exist together.

You can have big audacious goals, and you can be content with what you have today. Desire and contentment can exist together.

You can be sad when life's hard, but also grateful because of life's lessons, they made you stronger, they gave you abs of steel!

Sadness and gratitude can exist together.

You can be working towards a million-dollar brand, but still be proud closing your next dream client, and enjoy every step of progress you're making towards that journey.1 percent improvement is all we want to aspire for. (courtesy: James Clear, Atomic Habits)

You can be scared of making that investment in a big mastermind, but still take the leap while being nervous, scared and positively giddy of the transformation that's coming.

In all these moments in my life, I always think about how much darkness and light can exist together. Is one necessarily greater than the other? We always pursue light. But we need to go through a dark night to appreciate the morning light. The full moon on a pitch-dark night makes it all the more gorgeous, potent and soothing. Will light have any meaning without darkness? Why are we scared of darkness? Will not success taste sweeter because of how hard it all was? When everything is said and done, won't we want to be deserving of it, instead of our desires just being handed to us?

Lie: You need to wait for the perfect timing

You will not magically transition and wake up an overnight success.

I have wanted to write a book since I was a kid. Did I have perfect timing? Of course not. For years I thought, I should become a responsible CEO and focus on running and growing my company; and that writing will amount to nothing. But if you have a dream, you have to make time out for it.

No one is going to beg you to write.

No one is going to beg you to produce that music album. No one is going to beg you to release your coaching program.

No one is going to beg you to train hard and win that Olympic medal.

If you have a deep desire, you're going to have to make the time. I write when I can, even on sad frustrating days. I use the pain to write and create. I write even if I feel like I can't fit it into my daily schedule. I go on artist trips so I can hyperfocus on my art without distractions. Your dreams require work, effortlessness is a myth. No-one is going to come and force you to do the work. You have to be disciplined to start and keep at it despite challenges.

It was the same set of motivations when I was running my travel blog while working at my software engineering job. Nobody asked me to do it. Nobody begged me to start posting on social media. I learnt how to create a website, how to take pretty pictures, and how to write blogs. And all that helped me create my own online education and marketing company. This was nine years ago. I haven't done any travel blogging in a while but it led to the start of everything I do now. Don't wait for the perfect timing, start now. *Start today.*

You have to make time out of it. Even if it's an hour every day after your day job. Or half a day during the weekend. You might have to spend less time with your family or sacrifice some sleep. You have the same hours in the day as Taylor Swift. Make it count.

You don't get to keep everything as is and still be able to achieve your dreams. You don't get to keep partying with friends, or spend your weekends being drunk, or sleep late, binging Netflix every night, and still achieve every dream of yours. That's not how it works. But you can have the things you want, if you can practice living and working intentionally. Every good thing takes time so learn to be patient with yourself too.

In this book, I have given you all the tools in my kit, everything that has helped me till date. I look forward to meeting you someday, and you telling me how this book has helped you. I look forward to us learning together in my courses or masterminds someday.

I am rooting so hard for you to become wealthy and start making moves for it today.

Acknowledgments

Thank you mom, for bringing me into the world. When I was very young, I wanted to become an artist, an astronaut, an author, a teacher, a scientist—and so many other things. Thank you for harbouring a belief within me that I can do anything and be anything in this world. Your kindness, grace and unconditional love inspires me every single day.

Thank you dad, for putting in countless hours to teach me math and science; for being there for the debate practices, for checking my school progress every day, for pushing me to do sports, for the countless small things I'm forgetting now, and for always encouraging me. Your resilience and tenacity inspire me daily.

Thank you Rachit, for being my cheerleader, sounding board, best friend, travel bestie, partner in crime, and a wall through all my ups and downs for the last 14 years. And for saving me from flunking algebra in college!

To Kavya, my best friend and forever cheerleader, we have the best time giggling and cackling like hyenas. Our inside jokes are my favourite and I love you so much—I'm so proud of the woman you're becoming.

To Taylor Swift, the artist, the writer, and the hard worker that you are. Your songs, the grainy Eras tour live streams, the Eras Tour Singapore shows gave me life and were a huge motivator for me to complete this book. Thank you for showing me that karma is my boyfriend and that trash always takes itself out. Ha!

To Enid Blyton, Carolyn Keene, Agatha Christie, JK Rowling for writing countless books that I devoured as a lonely, introverted, bespectacled kid.

Thank you to my early book readers who believed in me and the book, you guys kept me going!

A huge shoutout to Anushree Majumdar, my editor, who worked with me for months to turn this book into something I'm proud to put in your hands. To Shreya Ahlawat at Bound for managing the project timelines and logistics. And to my lovely designer, Pranita Kocharekar for bringing my vision to life with the book cover.

To all my mastermind clients, private clients and course customers, thank you for trusting me and supporting me every step of the way.

Thank you to me, for not giving up on this book project for the past five years. And for believing in myself enough to get it finally done. We did it, Roo! The story is out of my system now, and it's yours to do with it what you will.

To you my reader and wealth movers, I love you and I'm rooting for you.

Roota

About The Author

Roota Mittal is an award-winning thought leader on business and financial empowerment. She has created a million-dollar education brand that now serves thousands of clients and students across 15 countries. She is best known for her popular digital courses and coaching programs, her ongoing mastermind for entrepreneurs looking to scale up, and for creating a community of over 4,000 high-achieving entrepreneurs whom she has mentored.

Roota's mission is to empower people to achieve greater freedom and wealth through online education via digital products, high-end group coaching, and 1:1 consulting offers. She helps small businesses acquire the tools, marketing expertise, and strategies needed to grow in today's AI-focused world through social media and advertising. She is passionate about helping women gain economic power and increase their earnings. With over 10 years of experience working with six-and seven-figure entrepreneurs, her proven sales process, social media strategies, and Meta Ads expertise have generated more than $16 million in client sales and counting.

Her work has been featured in *Forbes USA and HuffPost.* Her company is a recipient of the ClickFunnels 2 Comma Club award. Roota holds a Bachelor's degree in Computer Science from the Dhirubhai Ambani Institute of Information and

Communication Technology, India.

Born and raised in Gujarat, India, she has run her business from various parts of the world. She currently resides in Dubai with her husband.

You can find her at *rootamittal* on Instagram.

Go to her website *https://learnwithroota.com* to learn from her digital programs, work closely with her inside her mastermind and check out her best resources to keep your wealthy moves journey going.

www.ingramcontent.com/pod-product-compliance
Lightning Source LLC
Chambersburg PA
CBHW050523240926
51846CB00003B/667
9789334262445